THE WORD *of* MY TESTIMONY

LANCE WATSON

authorHOUSE®

AuthorHouse™
1663 Liberty Drive
Bloomington, IN 47403
www.authorhouse.com
Phone: 1 (800) 839-8640

Published by AuthorHouse 02/02/2016

ISBN: 978-1-5049-7808-8 (sc)
ISBN: 978-1-5049-7733-3 (e)

CONTENTS

CH. 1

THE LORD'S CALL

Jesus Christ The God-Man

Out of Glory
Christ descended,
clothing Himself in human skin.
Through a virgin girl
He entered our world
to redeem His bride from sin.

In His Flesh
Christ revealed
the Will of His Father to fallen man.
Begotten from above,
matchless in His love,
He's the cornerstone of God's redemption plan.

In the Spirit
Christ defeated
sin, death and the wicked one.
They bruised His heel,
His blood they spilled,
but death bowed down to the Risen Son.

Unto Glory
Christ ascended
to prepare a place for His Own.
At His Father's side,
He awaits His bride,
to share with her His Heavenly home.

*   *   *

The Making Of A Holy Bride

Conceived
in an eternal heart.
Souls
nurtured in the womb
of Holiness;
sustained by
the elixir
of Diving Passion.
A beautiful woman
kissed into being
by
The Sovereign One.

A gift
from the Eternal One,
snatched away.
A blessing
of inconceivable wonders,
twisted
into a curse
of unfathomable horrors
by
"I will."

The divine gene,
mutated.
The everlasting
broken

into little pieces
of time.
Moments
now priceless,
even desperate,
windows of opportunity.
Tragically,
most remain shut.

Adam and Eve,
miraculous mirrors
designed
to reflect God's glory,
become
dark and gnarled shadows.

Spirits,
engineered to sing
in harmony with
The Holy Spirit,
scream
their own sounds
of dissonance.
They screech
in rhythm to
"I will."

But
in a valley
there was a
Lilly.
In the land of Sharon
there was a
Rose.
This Lilly,

this Rose,
so perfect in beauty and grace,
attracted
a dove from Heaven.
Upon the head
of an Innocent One,
weaved into
His curly locks,
the dove
found
The Lilly
and
The Rose.

This innocent One,
so full of sorrows,
knelt
in a garden.
His sweat,
blood-red with fervor.
His heart
pulsing,
bursting
with a love
that
would slay Him.

His lips
uttering words
to
The Sovereign One,
"Not as I will,
but as You will."

He arose
from his knees,
impaled Himself
to a tree,
and
embraced the world.

Out of His wounds,
poured blood.
Out of His blood,
poured life.
And
out of Himself
He brought forth
His bride.

*   *   *

The Bible

The Bible,
simply put,
is a road map
charting the course
from earth to heaven,
from death to life,
from time to eternity.
The course is blood-splattered,
bearing the footprints
of the God-Man,
The Christ,
JESUS

*   *   *

Soul Hunter

Before I was born, God set my goal,
to seek out the lost soul.
As a Soul Hunter am I called,
to rescue victims of the fall.

No human training have I received;
my Trainer and Captain is The Trinity.
He sends me to the darkest parts,
where fear grips the captive heart.

In secret I go to the hidden place,
where sinners hide from Heaven's Grace.
Boldly I enter the regions of hell
to speak The Word against Satan's spell.

Wherever I'm sent, demons flee,
fearing the Christ who reigns in me.
Like Philip in Acts, so am I,
imbued with power from On High.

The power in me is not my own;
it flows from God's Heavenly Throne.
No personal glory do I seek;
"Jesus is Lord!" is what I speak.

Flanked by angels on either side,
The Holy Spirit within me resides.
No power on earth can thwart my way;
walls fall down whenever I pray.

Satan fights as such a frenzied pace,
knowing he's about to lose his place.
His demons shoot their fiery darts,
but my shield of faith guards my heart.

Awesome adventures have I known,
as I team with God to redeem His own.
Many a soul we snatch from the fire,
souls held fast by sin's desire.

Few there be who walk this path,
ever fearful of Satan's wrath.
But those found faithful in this endeavor
will surely shine like the stars forever.

So hear me well demon and man,
in God's presence do I stand.
I tread behind enemy lines
to free the soul that Satan binds.

This war I'll fight until the end;
through me God's Kingdom will extend.
My resolve is sure, my passion great;
my mission ends at Heaven's gates.

A Soul Hunter from my birth,
thus I sojourn in the earth.
No greater calling can there be
than to introduce you to The Trinity.

*   *   *

The Great Commission

God used men like the writer uses a pen;
thus He recorded His truth.
Obey His Word, your prayers will be heard,
and your life will bear much fruit.

From your early days, learn of His ways,
and fix your eyes on Christ.
Humble your heart, from evil depart,
and The Holy Spirit will guide your life.

Reflect God's Glory, proclaim Christ's Story,
and many souls will be won.
Rescue the lost, take them to The Cross,
where they'll bathe in the the blood of the Son.

Reject Satan's lies, in God's Truth abide;
defending the faith at all times.
Be bold in Christ, displaying His life,
and like the stars you will forever shine.

Do not be ashamed to herald His Name
despite the obstacles sent your way.
God is faithful to protect His Holy Elect,
and powerfully responds whenever we pray.

We all have a place in this time of Grace
that conforms to His Holy Plan.
He who endures God surely rewards,
but the fearful shall not stand.

We will be opposed by the Lord's foes,
for we are engaged in a holy war.
We are Heaven's saints and shall not be faint;
the Word of God is our sword.

The hour is late and hell awaits
the soul that Satan blinds.
We have our task and must stand fast,
while the Lord still grants us time.

It is Satan's hour but do not cower,

for the war is already won.
Know this my friend, we are at the end,
and our work will soon be done.

*   *   *

Divine Fishermen

He called upon men,
twelve in all.
Eleven served faithfully,
but one did fall.

They left family and friends
for this unknown stranger.
He had neither fame nor wealth,
and was born in a manger.

The first four called
were fishermen of the sea.
Unto them said Jesus,
"Come and cast your nets for Me.

I will teach you to fish,
like you've never known before.
If you only welcome Me
when I knock at your door.

For I too am a Fisherman,
possessing divine skill.
You will fish for souls
and have powers to heal.

But all you receive
is given with a price.
You must deny yourselves,
and surrender to My might.

Into a den of wolves
shall you go as sheep.
Teaching and ministering
to the souls who weep.

Have no concern
for your own sustenance.
The Father provides for all
who seek His guidance.

Go preach the Good News
for all to hear.
Jesus Christ is Lord,
and His Kingdom is near."

*   *   *

The Gospel

I turn my back on this world of sin,
so seductively calling my name.
Come Holy Spirit and dwell within
this temple flawed by sin and shame.

Only by Christ can a life so evil
transform into a beacon of light.
Out of darkness come forth a people,
washed in the blood of Jesus Christ.

God came down clothed in skin,
and entered into a virgin's womb.
On a cursed cross He bore our sins,
and left death dying in an empty tomb.

Christ ascended to His Father's throne
to prepare our place for eternity.
He'll soon return to gather His own,
and judge the works of his enemies.

With joy I await my Lord's return,
but still there's an ache in my soul.
In a lake of fire many shall burn
for rejecting The One the prophets foretold.

Take heed, my friend, whoever you are,
and receive the Gift of salvation.
Kiss the One called The Morning Star,
and He'll love you out of damnation.

*   *   *

God's Warrior

He's just a mere man in this world,
but a fierce warrior behind the veil.
He boldly invades the dark regions,
freeing souls from Satan's spell.

In spiritual armor he wages war,
this saint of a rare kind.
Majestic angels pave the way,
as he treads behind enemy lines.

The Lord Himself trained this one
to rescue souls from the fire.
Bringing the lost to the blood-stained cross,
is the warrior's prime desire.

This warrior possesses divine skills,
honed throughout the years.
Stealthily he invades Satan's camp,
casting aside all human fear.

Exclusively deployed on one-man missions,
this rare warrior walks a lonely path.
His eye is focused on The Lord alone,
and he fears not Satan's wrath.

Quietly The Lord directs his spirit,
and usually with little time to spare.
The warrior must heed that Quiet Voice,
alerting him to satanic snares.

Scores of demons seek his blood,
hoping to claim the great reward.
But the warrior wields a shield of faith,
and his bible is a double-edged sword.

He's at the top of Satan's hit-list,
and his victories come with a price.
In his soul he bears many wounds,
wounds that shout "Glory!" to Jesus Christ.

At times he's faltered in his walk,
and Satan struck a fiery blow.
But the Lord honored his contrite heart,
and upon the warrior, His Grace flows.

But now the warrior's end draws near,
for his Lord has drawn a line.
Soon the warrior will meet his Lord,
and in Heaven his crown will forever shine.

*   *   *

Call To War

Decades ago my heart said "Yes!"
to the beckoning call of Lord Jesus.
My sins were cleansed in the Blood of the Lamb;
on Holy ground, I stood a new man.

Unable to reach Him, God stooped down,
and placed on my head a royal crown.
Grace snatched me from the blazing fire,
and birthed in me a most holy desire.

The Holy Spirit began to teach me;
"The truth, He said, will set you free."
The armor of God, He gave me to wear;
"Satan and his demons you need not fear."

Clothed in His armor, I was sent to fight,
accompanied by fierce angels of might.
Boldly we invade the regions of hell,
freeing souls from Satan's cells.

The angels and I fight valiantly,
following the commands of The Trinity.
The armies of darkness grow forlorn
whenever the angel blows his horn.

The Kingdom of Heaven gains much ground
as the armies of God fight world-round.
His Glorious Kingdom will continue to extend
and Satan's rebellion will surely end.

Wounds I have from this relentless war,
but they will heal at Heaven's door.
Though tired and weary, I continue to fight,
for my Savior's cause is my delight.

So hearken, my friend, to His call;
in Him you, too, will stand tall.
The time is short, do not delay.
Hear His voice and be quick to obey.

*   *   *

His Voice

I hear a voice
in my quiet mind;
a voice so gentle,
a voice so divine.

Such a quiet voice
can scarce be heard,
amidst the noisy sounds
and discordant words.

One would think
that a God so great
would speak in thunders,
and the world would shake.

Yet when the soul
is calm and still,
softly God speaks
His purpose and Will.

As He once spoke peace
to a raging sea,
likewise He calms
the tempest within me.

The ear does not hear
God speaking to the soul.
Whenever He speaks,
marvelous truths unfold.

Beware of the impostor,
though his words be sweet.
Believing his lies
precedes a fiery leap.

God never contradicts
what His bible declares.
Test every word
and avoid the snares.

When once you hear
His celestial voice,
speaking daily with Him
will be your fervent choice.

*   *   *

I am The Called

Anoint me Lord to write for Thee,
allow me to be your pen.
Open my eyes that I might see
your Spirit move in the lives of men.

Give me the words that I should speak,
and the boldness to tell your story.
Give me a spirit not proud but meek,
for only then will I see your glory.

I am yours and not my own;
I offer my gifts for your pleasure.
May my motives please your will alone,
and my works gain eternal treasures.

I've lived for me entirely too long,
and have wasted much that you gave.
I've walked in the ways of a worldly throng,
who blindly race to a God-less grave.

You were gracious to bring to an end
the foolish path upon which I tread.
In your fiery furnace my ways you amend,
and in time you will exalt my head.

Behold, I see the day drawing near
when Satan will make his final stand.
Through his powers to deceive and incite fear,
he ushers in the destruction of man.

But you have promised to reserve a remnant,
and destroy the plans of the wicked one.
For by your blood we have a new covenant,
and the war we face is already won.

Unto Thee, my Lord, I give my all
for the sake of the battles ahead.
For by thy grace, I am the called,
and daily I declare my flesh is dead.

*   *   *

Glimpses Of Soul Winning

He sat alone in the noisy bar,
haunted by painful memories.
The door to his future was slightly ajar,
and I glimpsed his fate in eternity.

My Lord said "Enter this place,
for I business with that one."
Deep despair was etched in his face,
but The Spirit said "He's ready to come."

He looked at me through curious eyes,
wondering why he felt drawn to me.
In his darkened soul he didn't realize
that he was about to encounter The Trinity.

The voice weeping through the phone
was filled with pain and despair.
Her husband left her all alone
with three babies in her care.

Her broken voice had an irritating whine,
which made me weary listening to her.
My Lord said "Give her your time,
for I'm sending you as My messenger."

She questioned why the Lord hides
in her season of painful calamity.
"My works are good and I never lie,
so why does God treat me as an enemy?"

The Lord said "Speak of my grace,
and that works fall short of the mark.
Her works will lead her to a fiery place,
but I reside in the believing heart."

*　　*　　*

I missed the train and wondered why
my angel allowed me to sleep.
The Spirit said "You must here abide,
for there's a prodigal son for you to meet."

I saw him coming, this prodigal son,
all beat-down by the world.
The Spirit said "He's at the end of his fun,
and we're here because of a praying girl."

The Spirit said "Offer him a light,
then ask him about his cross.
If in his answer he mentions Christ,
explain to him the fate of the lost."

Intrigued by this, I hastened to obey,
and did as the Spirit said.
It was clear to me that he lost his way,
when he spoke these words with bowed head:

"My dad believed in Jesus Christ,
and wore this cross till the day he died.
I'm so ashamed of my wasted life,
and if Dad could see me, he'd surely cry."

My Lord spoke saying "Bring him to me,"
and the Spirit anointed my tongue.
As we prayed, he wept bitterly,
while the angel sang "Another soul is won."

*   *   *

Alone she laid in the hospital room;
her life and body ravaged by sin.
Her hopes were slain by relentless gloom,
and condemning voices from without and within.

Hours, maybe days, was all that remained
of a life gone horribly amiss.
She dared to hope that in death she'd gain
a final chance at eternal bliss.

In a distant place a weary man prayed
for a daughter he lost long ago.
With a heavy heart on his knees he stayed,
until the grace of God from heaven flowed.

God heard the prayers of this faithful father,
and quickly sent His angel to me.
The angel spoke of a long lost daughter
who would soon enter eternity.

Urgently the angel spoke to my mind,
and led me to the dying girl.
There she laid, spiritually blind,
desperately afraid of leaving this world.

As I held her hand and spoke of Christ,
pent-up tears flowed down her face.
I explained that, for her, Jesus gave his life,
and all her sins His blood will erase.

The angel's wings overshadowed us,
as we bowed our heads to pray.
She whispered the prayer "Lord Jesus
come into my heart and forever stay."

*   *   *

There was a jubilant man in a distant place,
dancing and singing before God's Throne.
The Lord told him "Go now in haste,
for your beloved daughter is ready to come home.

*   *   *

Ode To Persecuted Saints

No mega Churches, fortune or fame
for persecuted saints in hostile lands.
"Jesus Is Lord" is what they proclaim,
despite Satan's murderous plans.

Homes are destroyed and families broken,
because they preach the gospel.
Out of their mouths the truth is spoken,
saving the souls of lost people.

These persecuted saints have no fear,
though many must stand alone.
They endure torture while the wicked cheer,
but God watches from His heavenly Throne.

Some are killed while others escape,
still they're faithful to Jesus Christ.
Children are murdered and wives raped,
so extreme is their sacrifice.

Muslims and Hindus filled with hate,
boldly assault them without restraint.
Evil governments gladly forsake
their duty to protect these innocent saints.

Many struggle to provide for their families,
when their jobs are taken away.
Yet they still show love to their enemies,
and for their souls they fervently pray.

But God has provided many loving hands
to minister to these persecuted saints.
He raised up followers of Richard Wurmbrand,
who tirelessly minister without complaint.

They provide food, bibles and even homes,
to the saints who have been displaced.
God guides them from His heavenly Throne,
and showers them in Heaven's Grace.

The saints in America must join this fight,
by doing and giving whatever we can.
Through our prayers and gifts we strongly unite
with the followers of Richard Wurmbrand.

Do not delay, tomorrow's too late
to put our hands to the task.
Soon we will face a similar fate,
so now is the time to pray and fast.

*   *   *

Precious Love

You loved me from afar off,
and claimed me as your own.
Your precious love I dared to scoff,
and told you to leave me alone.

You left your throne to rescue me
by clothing yourself in flesh.
I wanted to seek my own destiny,
convinced my way was best.

You left your glory in heaven above
to amend man's eternal blunder.
You demonstrated your steadfast love
through acts of miraculous wonder.

You healed me of my sickness,
and called me out of the tomb.
Pride remained my deadly weakness
that threatened to seal my doom.

You sought me in my hiding place,
and called to me from the temple.
You poured upon me amazing grace,
and healed so many people.

Yet still my heart was hardened,
and I refused to let you in.
Despite this you offered to pardon,
and free me from the wages of sin.

Then I saw the rage of the Pharisees
as they looked upon you in fear.
You boldly exposed their hypocrisy,
knowing your rebuke drew death near.

Suddenly my heart began to turn
as your words resonated in my mind.
Your holiness made my soul yearn
to belong to One so divine.

I searched for you in all the land
that I might kneel at your feet.
The burning inside I didn't understand,
but I knew that my heart was yours to keep.

Not finding you made me despair,
and I fell on my knees and cried.
Then I heard a voice inside my ear
telling me you were about to die.

The voice led me to that wooden cross,
where your life poured out like a flood.
You looked upon me as one who was lost,
and whispered "For you I shed my blood."

I knelt where your body hung
with tears flowing from my eyes.
At that cross my new life begun,
and my wicked ways I now despised.

On the third day you rose from the dead,
and appear to all who so believe.
I'm eternally grateful for the blood you shed
out of a precious love for a wretch like me.

*   *   *

CH. 2

IT IS NOT GOOD FOR MAN TO BE ALONE

Enduring Love

The essence of spiritual affinity,

and the invisible manifestation of enduring love

is realized in the ability

to see one another in the light of darkness;

to speak with one another in a dialogue of silence;

to feel one another without touching;

to find ecstasy without searching;

to grasp the heights without reaching;

to know one another without asking questions;

to grow through one another without possessing;

to allow space between one another without fearing;

to pursue different dreams while walking the same path;

to descend into the valleys without accusing;

to rise from the valleys without separating;

to ascend the highest mountain without forgetting;

to share your last sunset with your hearts still tightly embracing.

(For Dori)

*   *   *

When The Lord Created Thee

When the Lord created thee,
He thought for a moment of me.
When He sculpted your delicate face,
He traced the curve of the palm of my hand.
When He fashioned the exquisite dimensions of your body,
He conformed them to the contours of my own.
When He colored your skin with the brightness of the sun,
He smiled at my sad longing when I first beheld beauty.
When He crowned you with flowing strands of black silk,
He considered my fascination for the mysterious and exotic.
When He anointed you with sweet odors of innocence,
He added a pinch of that special fragrance
that so naturally captivates me.
When He breathed upon your lips to awaken your life,
He numbered my days of wandering in loneliness.

When The Lord Created Thee, He Thought For a Moment of Me.

When He placed pleasure at the threshold of your soul,
He smiled as He etched my silhouette into
the fibers of your emotions.
When He refined you with patience and tolerance,
He was mindful of the recklessness with which I attacked life.
When He weaved gentleness and peace into your eternal character,
He laughed as He heard the death-cry of my brittle heart.
When His tear pierced your heart that you might know sorrow,
He remembered my laughter, my strength and my love.
When He covered your nakedness with His Glorious Righteousness,
He answered my silent prayer that my eye may behold Him.
When He sealed-up the sum of your heart,
He reserved the inner chamber for His own dwelling.
But He carved out a niche and,
with fire,
He engraved my name thereto.

*   *   *

A Single Destiny

For so many years,
too many years,
from the distance,
and in silence,
I loved thee.

You were,
to me,
an endless dream,
a hopeless desire;
a shameful,
yet shameless,
unspeakable yearning.
I caressed
your image,
your shadow,
but never your flesh.

From the hidden place,
I observed you
intently;
studied you
fervently.
But
out of mercy
for my very own soul,
I avoided you.

Your golden beauty,
so irrepressibly transcendent,

so captivating,
made you shy.
Instead of
flaunting your beauty,
you tried
to hide it,
repress it,
and blend with the ordinary.
But can the sun
hide it's brilliance
behind shadows,
or blend with the night?
Your natural scent,
untainted by perfume,
intoxicated me.
Your voice
calmed the storm
within me,
and made my soul
yearn.

Your rare laughter
was like the sound
of angels rejoicing.
Your soul,
so quietly vibrant,
so subtly passionate,
yet so lonely,
beckoned me
in silent whispers.

In anguish,
with shame,
yet without shame,
I spoke of you,

of me,
of us,
to The Father.

Though forbidden,
thus I prayed:
"Lord,
if it be at all possible,
for however short the time,
or long,
give me this woman."

In a whisper,
He thus answered:
"You and the woman
shall share
a single destiny."

Ten years later,
when hope
sang no more,
when life became
a mere tolerance;
when loneliness
held us close at night,
and sorrow
awakened us
to the inevitable
and dreadful morning,
God
merged our destinies.

Two hearts,
so full of sorrow,
so full of unfulfilled love,

became a single,
living,
loving organism.
God placed
this divinely ordained loving organism,
in the midst of His palm.
Then,
in the presence of our angels,
The Lord spoke
His blessing,
and then gently
clenched His fist.

*   *   *

CH. 3

FAMILY
A BLESSING AND A CURSE

Dad

I remember my Dad as big and strong,
very loving in a quiet, gentle way.
He tried to teach us right from wrong,
and worked hard till he died one day.

I was only ten when my Dad died,
and I remember the day so clear.
I remember how Mom bitterly cried,
and my own feelings of utter fear.

Dad's love for Mom was so very deep,
despite her adulterous ways.
I remember the nights he didn't sleep,
and her bottles he threw away.

He tried so hard to make things work,
yet his face rarely wore a smile.
I didn't know how much he hurt,
because sharing pain wasn't his style,.

There were many things I didn't realize,
but I remember feeling sorry for Dad.
I could look deep into his sad brown eyes,
and see sorrow for the troubles we had.

I remember he once spoke of divorce,
and I pleaded for him to take me.
But even as I pleaded I saw his remorse
because Dad had a heart for family.

He never spoke of divorce again,
but he rarely spent time at home.
I always felt in my soul his pain,
and without him I felt so alone.

Now that thirty years have gone by
I can write a poem for my Dad.
Yet even as I write I begin to cry,
cause I still feel the pain he had.

But my tears are not for Dad alone,
because now I too have a family.
Like Dad I don't spend much time at home,
for those whom I love resent me.

Strange, but like Dad I have two sons,
and I'm deeply in love with my wife.
Like Dad I see love in my youngest one,
but with the others there's only strife.

So Dad your story has become mine,
and I bear your so-sad legacy.
Our curse has become one of a kind,
but in heaven we'll know ecstasy.

But I'm not certain if you were saved,
and it's too late to pray for you.
In heaven or hell in my heart you will stay,
and I'm glad for ten years my Dad I knew.

(I will always remember and love you Dad.
Please be there Dad; be there).

*   *   *

Angry Fruit

What a misery,
her tortured journey through life;
what a tale of woe.
A harbinger
of all kinds of strife;
the angry fruit
of lust sowed.

Orphan of shame,
left unclaimed.
Her home,
a corner somewhere.
Took for herself
a stranger's name,
and drank
to drown her despair.

A gentleman's touch
she never knew;
deceived
by passions of the flesh.
Her good Samaritans,
way too few;
her search for love,
a pitiful quest.

Her sensuous beauty,
she soon realized,
was like a wand
that could open locked doors.
She was easy prey
in Satan's eyes,
but deaf
to the call of the Lord.

Too young
to out-slick
the slicker boys,
her quest
gave birth to a child.
This fruit of lust
stifled her joy,
and she only kept the baby
for a while.

Three times more
she repeated the mistake,
but with a prince
who had a gentleman's touch.
Her prince discovered,
entirely too late,
that his wife's crippled heart
could only love so much.

But the prince's heart
was bound to his wife,
despite her destructive ways.
And he kept his vows
for the rest of his life,
then he died
brokenhearted
one day.

Deeper she sank
into her hellish world,
ensnared by all kinds of sin.
But while in a stupor
a scared little girl
cried out to God
from deep within.

A bullet to her head
and a death-dose of pills
couldn't silence
the little girl's voice.
At a time when her soul
was calm and still,
Someone whispered to the girl,
"My Blood is still moist."

She lifted her heart
to the voice from above
and cried,
"I have nothing more to give."
The God-Man appeared,
His heart bursting with love,
and spoke to her soul,
"your sins I forgive."

When her angel came
to escort her home,
a little girl's smile
was etched on her face.
I stood by her side
for a moment alone,
and knew that
my mother
found the Gift of Grace.

*　　*　　*

No More!

No more
eruptions of pain
searing emotional and spiritual
nerves.
No more
twisted knots in a stomach
that abhors food.

No more
middle-of-the-night
awakenings,
drenched in cold sweat
and hot tears.

No more
slumped shoulders
and vacant stares.
No more
clenched fists
and bitter questions
that God
absolutely refuses to answer.

A broken heart
eventually becomes a cold heart.

No more
reflections
of my little boys' face
in the eyes
of every child passing by.
No more
pangs of guilt
when I gaze at a picture
of my tortured and tormented
teenage son,
lost in a world of darkness
and self-destruction.

No more
counting of the days
when
I last held her
and
heard her sweet voice
whisper
"I love you."

No more
fervent prayers
uttered from the depths
of a desperate spirit,
pleading
for the healing
of a deeply wounded family.

No more
disappointments
when those fervent prayers
bounce off
a cold ceiling
and fall dead
at my worn knees.

A broken heart
eventually becomes a cold heart.

*   *   *

What If?

It's been so long,
use to be too long;
use to be.
Heart doesn't ache,
not even silently,
for you anymore.

Still,
at times I wonder:

What if
we would've fought
for us
instead of
against us,
for one more day?

What if
we would've forgave
one more insult;
overlooked
one more offense?
What if
we would've held our tongue
for just one more hour?

What if,
on that last night,
we would've said
one more urgent prayer
instead of shouting
one last wicked curse?

What if
we would've tried
to out-do each other
with kindness
instead of
with vindictiveness?

What if
we would've said
"Let's try again"
instead of
"Good-bye?"

What if
we would've believed,
and not doubted,
for just
one more hour?

What if
we would've thought
of the children
instead of
'Me?'

What if
you would've left
for just one more day
instead of
forever?

What if
we would've focused
on Christ
and His word
"And they shall be one flesh"
for just one more hour?

*   *   *

CH. 4

SPIRITUAL WARFARE
AND
THE CHALLENGES
OF CHRISTIANITY

The Last Saint

I awoke with an eerie feeling that day,
which filled me with anxiety.
I knelt to my knees and began to pray,
sensing an imminent catastrophe.

Soon the Lord began to speak to me,
and showed me the face of a boy.
The boy was in the midst of evil company,
who stole his innocence and joy.

I asked the Lord "What shall I do,
and why have you shown me this face?"
God said "Go, for the moments are few,
and he's the last saint in this age of grace."

Then the Lord revealed an awesome sight
that made my heart feel faint.
Innumerable angels were arrayed in flight
with their eyes fixed on the last saint.

The Spirit led me to dark place in the city
where Satan and his demons dwell.
Knowing my mission, Satan cursed The Trinity,
and vowed to send the boy to hell.

The darkness of the city was densely black,
and it's dwellers were wickedly cruel.
The Lord said "Let not your faith be slack,
for out of that darkness will come a jewel."

I passed through the crowd and sensed their hate,
for Satan had poisoned their hearts.
They were under the power of the chief reprobate,
and from his snare they'd never depart.

Satan and his demons surrounded me,
intent on taking my life.
I felt a pang of fear but refused to flee,
for I knew the power of Jesus Christ.

The angels chased Satan and his demons away,
and the people fled from a violent rain.
As I went for cover, I heard a voice say,
"Please help me sir, for I'm in pain."

When I saw his face, I let out a gasp,
and peered into his eyes for a while.
There he stood, the saint called last,
and all of heaven awaited this child.

As quickly as it came, the storm abated,
and alone with God stood the boy and I.
This thin little saint, so emaciated,
clung to me and began to cry.

The love of Christ flowed through me,
and I held him tight in my arms.
This last saint would soon be free,
and no more fear the devil's harm.

As a babe, he said, he was stolen from home,
and forced to commit despicable acts.
"In this darkness I've suffered all alone,
and every good thing my soul lacks."

I explained to him the love of Christ,
and that for us He willingly died.
Through His blood He grants eternal life,
and for this reason He was crucified.

Open your heart and welcome Him in,
and He will love all of your pain away.
His blood will cleanse you from every sin,
and with Him in heaven you'll stay.

He began to weep and confess his sin,
but wondered if God truly loved him.
His doubt left when Christ entered in
and opened his eyes to see the cherubim.

In awe I watched in reverent amazement,
but wondered why I received this task.
As the boy reveled in ecstatic contentment,
my Lord said "You need only to ask."

So I asked God why I was chosen
to bring the last saint to His Throne.
He said "Years ago your son was stolen
from the love and safety of your home.

You thought this day would never come,
yet still you served me without restraint.
This day have I reunited father and son,
    for your stolen boy is the last saint."

I took my son into my loving arms,
and weeping and laughing we fell to the ground.
Then suddenly we heard a piercing alarm,
    like that of a trumpet battle sound,.

The sky receded behind a glorious light
    that lit up the entire planet.
Angels were escorting the Bride of Christ,
    as Gabriel blew his rapturous trumpet.

My son and I were the last ones to rise,
    as a legion of angels escorted us.
Satan and his minions were left terrorized,
    as the last saint soared to Jesus.

*   *   *

Prepare

Time is racing, demons chasing,
the world is in despair.
By design it's Satan's time;
saints are being prepared.

Heed His word, prayers are heard;
don't believe the lies.
To open ears, the truth is clear;
wolves are in disguise.

The Lord's bride walks a holy stride,
spotless in her flowing white gown.
Like her Groom divine, her glory shines,
breathless in her glory-studded crown.

Scriptures warning, fools scorning,
Christ will soon return.
Open ye graves, release the saved,
but the lost will surely burn.

The hour is late, storm hell's gates,
snatching souls from the fire.
Seeing the lost at the foot of the Cross
is The Trinity's prime desire.

We are the Church, the salt of the earth;
who can stand against us?
By The Holy Ghost and with the heavenly hosts,
we proclaim the name of Jesus.

There's a trumpet sound heard world-round;
it's Gabriel blowing his horn.
The saints rise to the fearful surprise
of those who dared to scorn.

So lift up your eyes, behold the skies;
see the angels in flight.
The clouds part, the rapture starts;
behold the glorious sight!

*   *   *

Flesh vs Spirit

(Ro.7:19)

I like my lanes
fast and smooth,
and my direction straight ahead.
But I find the lanes are,
sometimes,
too fast,
and straight ahead,
sometimes,
follows U-turns.
I like my lights green;
but yellow makes me reflect,
and red makes me give
others an opportunity.

I like my skies
clear and bright,
with few scattered clouds.
But I only see the beauty
of a rainbow
after a storm.
I love the brightness
of the sun,
and feeling it's warm breath
against my skin.
But the beauty and brilliance
of the stars
are only visible
in the darkness of night.

I like my woman
just the way she is.
Yet my eye still roams.

I like my moods
calm.
But an inner tempest
often betrays me.
I like being patient,
but rarely am.
I'm passionate
about serving God.
But carnality,
too often,
preempts my passion.

I like sin,
and hate liking it.

I hate Satan,
but sometimes
I taste his candy.
The taste is sweet
in my mouth,
but bitter
in my stomach.

I love Jesus
pulling my strings,
even though,
sometimes,
I pull back.

I like to count my friends
on one hand.
But the heart that loves all
imitates the Christ.
I like minding
my own business,
but caring for others
is the point of it all.
Imagine if Jesus said
"Find your own way."

I like redeeming the time,
but waste much of it.

I love talking to
The Father,
but rarely am I still,
knowing He is God.
I like God
seeing everything;
makes it real easy
being honest with Him.
Yet,
at times,
I wish He'd blink.

I love to worship God
in song and praises.
But often,
the greater worship,
in spirit and in truth,
gets lost somewhere
between flesh and spirit.

I like folks seeing Jesus
in me.
Yet,
way too often,
they only see
me.

I love reading the bible.
Although,
at times,
I avoid it
the way ugliness
avoids a mirror.

That which I loathe,
I do.
That which I desire to do,
I do not.

Flesh vs Spirit.
The quintessential,
relentless
conflict of life.

When the last breath
of life
is drawn,
and I soar into glory,
then,
and only then,
will this war
cease.

* * *

Backslidden

A saint's albatross.
An existence hovering
between
Heaven and Hell.
Too holy to blend
with the world;
too worldly to sit
in heavenly places.

It is loneliness
in a dark
and barren land.
A misery
that won't seek company;
the saints would be
contaminated,
the world would
mock.

Backslidden

It is the sun
hiding in shadows.
It is light
beaming rays of darkness.
It is peace
at war.

It is joy
mourning.
It is faith
doubting.

It is victory
cowering in defeat.

It is the spirit
reaching heavenward,
while the flesh
anchors it
to earth.

It is power
bowing to weakness.
It is the mind
not transformed;
gold unrefined.
It is the Holy Spirit
grieving.

Backslidden

It is the bible
dusty.
The prayer closet
empty.
The heart
not pliable.
The back
not bowed.

The knees
not bent.
The tongue
refusing to cry out
"Abba Father!"

It is the heart of Christ,
weeping,
and the pride of Satan
strutting.
It is Egypt
seducing,
then reclaiming.
It is wealth
choosing poverty.
It is freedom
re-embracing bondage.

Backslidden

It is the clay
wanting to be
the Potter,
and the Potter
granting the clay
it's wish.

It is the branch
withering
without the vine.
It is the prodigal
feeding with pigs;
the dog returning
to its' vomit.

It is Samson
forsaking
the call of a Nazirite
for pagan love.

It is King Saul
refusing to wait
for Samuel.

It is David's gaze
lingering too long
upon Uriah's rooftop.

It is the voices
of a thousand women
silencing the lyrics
of Solomon's Song.

It is Jonah
fleeing to Tarshish
with his back
facing Neneveh.

It is Peter
denying The Christ,
and Israel shouting
"Crucify Him!"

Backslidden

It is the key
that opens the door
to God's furnace;
therein He refines
His gold.

It is the one place
where the saint
personally discovers
that God is truly
married to the
backslidder.

*   *   *

Lost Joy

Such a sad and lonely soul
stirs restless within me.
Where are you my heavenly joy;
to where did you flee?

Seems like not long ago
we were such intimate friends.
We did everything together;
and together we'd be until the end.

Every morning you awakened me
with a soft kiss and gentle embrace.
Throughout the day we sang and danced,
as we reveled in His Grace.

With you residing in my heart,
my soul was deeply content.
You were a loyal and faithful friend;
a gift that was heaven sent.

Then one day I gazed too long
upon that which was forbidden me.
Oh how you desperately warned
that my flesh threatened our unity.

The Hand of Grace that held us bound,
released us from its' hold.
Sorrow and misery now reside
within the vacuum you left in my soul.

Now my days are spent in anguish,
as my soul mourns your loss.
When I chose to pursue my desire,
I failed to count the cost.

Will the Hand of Grace ever again
bring you back to me?
Will joy reunite with my soul,
and with my soul forever be?

*   *   *

Warning!

In the darkness of the night I saw a vision;
lo, strange craft were in the sky.
Demonic warriors were on a mission,
fulfilling the plan of the Most High.

People were scattering on the ground,
seeking refuge from the sword.
Mass destruction was all around,
as wrath drove the demonic horde.

The sun grew dark and the mood turned red,
as foretold by the prophets of old.
None could number the mounting dead;
no remedy left for the marked souls.

Fearful and battered, the nations fell
as victims of the Anti-Christ.
Nothing could stop this invasion from hell,
for they gain entrance through human vice.

Gold meant nothing to the poor or rich,
for the day of God's wrath is here.
None could redeem their soul from the pit,
for the Blood of Christ they dared to sneer.

The grace of God has come to an end,
extinguished by the murder of His saints.
God is coming as a judge, not a friend,
exacting His vengeance without restraint.

Unbridled horror is released upon man,
the likes of which he never knew.
God judges evil with a brutal hand,
an ancient truth, yet believed by few.

Tempt God no more with your evil way;
receive His Son and do well.
When His patience is done, God don't play,
and He will send you to a fiery hell.

*   *   *

In Christ, I Live

God tells me to wait,
and in Him be bold.
He'll soon elevate
my downcast soul.

As my tears flow,
they anoint my prayers.
And I surely know
that my Savior cares.

In my loneliness,
He's my companion.
He dispels the darkness
with loving communion.

In my pain,
He's my balm.
I praise His name,
and my soul is calm.

In my sorrow,
He's my smile.
Joy comes tomorrow,
so I endure for a while.

When I am weak,
He's my strength.
He will replete
the will that's spent.

When I feel guilt,
He removes the stain.
His blood is the quilt
that covers the shame.

When the enemy attacks,
God raises the standard.
He turns evil back,
and silences all slander.

When loved ones turn away,
my Lord remains.
He promises one day
heaven I'll gain.

When my faith falters,
I remember His Word.
I bow at His altar,
and my prayers are heard.

I don't trust what I feel
when trouble cascades.
He says "Peace be still,"
and the fear fades.

Waiting is strenuous,
but each moment is blessed.
He perfects righteousness
when my faith is tested.

* * *

Let God Arise

Ruthless days,
sleepless nights;
all around me
only strife.
When will God arise?

Forsaken by all,
none draw near.
Standing alone,
my soul in fear.
Satan's arrow found its' mark.

Sowed a kiss,
went too far.
Reaped a nightmare,
became a falling star.
Is my sin greater than Grace?

A hungry heart,
went astray.
Found her soul
and lost my way.
Will I ever find home again?

An Almighty Voice
called my name.
Fell to my knees;
couldn't bear the shame.
Will I rise from this dark pit?

What I thought
was so, so wrong.
What I felt
was way too strong.
Why were my prayers not answered?

Such a narrow path
I'm called to tread.
But the path I chose
walks the living dead.
O foolish saint am I.

One more chance
is all I need.
His Almighty Voice
I will surely heed.
Lord, don't let me die this way.

"Repent, repent!"
echoes in my mind.
"Your prayers are heard,
and your star will shine."
Behold, my God arises!

*   *   *

God's Rest

I go to bed with a heavy heart,
and arise with the same.
Joy is gone, my mood is dark,
but still I praise His name.

Another trial He sends my way
to test my faith in Him.
This bitter cup will empty one day,
so I dare not let hope dim.

During times such as these,
it's hard to feel His love.
It's the Lord whom I want to please,
as He watches me from above.

Sometimes my patience falters
when my pain is so great.
I bow myself at His altar,
and upon Him I choose to wait.

I know He sees my sorrow;
a contrite heart He holds dear.
My relief will come tomorrow,
and my way will be made clear.

At times my soul is so down-cast,
I can barely utter a prayer.
My trust in Christ remains steadfast,
lest I fall into Satan's snare.

Loved ones have forsaken me;
just God and I in this wilderness.
The Lord is faithful when others flee,
and in Him my soul finds rest.

*   *   *

.

My Spirit Speaks to My Soul

O hardened heart full of sin,
have you forgotten God?
The evil web that your mind spins
beckons His chastening rod.

Let His love replace your hate
before your hardness cements.
Wrath and anger quickly forsake
before you lose the will to repent.

Pain and sorrow poison your mind,
and let-downs quench your hope.
Within you dwells His Spirit Divine,
whose voice you dare not choke.

Open again the bible of truth,
and your faith will be revived.
Rejoice in the God of your youth,
for in your heart He still resides.

His heart aches with your pain,
and your tears fall from His Eye.
Remember the power of His Name,
and that for you He died.

You rejoice in sharing His eternal throne,
but cringe in the face of your cross.
You don't bear your burdens alone,
and He can restore what you have lost.

Each trial the Lord sends your way
is an exercise for your faith.
Trials are conquered when you pray,
and upon God patiently wait.

O my soul, hold firm my hand
as together we run this race.
My spirit is the new birth in man,
and together we will seek His Face.

Reaping

In this wretched flesh
I grieve the day long.
I'm desperate for heaven,
where there is no wrong.

My days have been too many
in this world of sin.
My guilt and shame
torments me from within.

Though I'm made righteous
by the Blood of Christ,
the sin and weight that besets me
shame His sacrifice.

My soul is sorely vexed
by my own disobedience.
My tongue expresses sorrow,
but where's the fruit of repentance?

The reaping I now endure
seems too great for me to bear.
The warnings of the Holy Spirit
were silenced by my deaf ear.

The many blessings that God bestowed
have virtually disappeared.
The song He put in my heart,
even that I no longer hear.

Friends have forsaken me,
and my pockets are full of holes.
The pursuit of forbidden love,
has brought me troubles untold.

The path I now walk,
my feet alone tread.
Though my heart still beats,
I walk among the dead.

I can't blame ignorance,
or lack of spiritual insight.
God taught me well His word,
but my flesh darkened it's light.

O sin, wretched, wretched sin,
how I delighted in you.
Now I count my days,
and beg God they be few.

*   *   *

There is Something About The Night

There is something about the night
that compels
the soul and spirit
to commune together
at their table of sorrow.

There is something about the night
that makes the heart of a fool merry,
and the heart of a wise one mourn.
That makes the peaceful one sleep,
and the troubled one weep.

There is something about the night
that unlocks the wellspring
of your deepest sorrows.
And,
like a flood,
your tears flow though,
perhaps,
you know not why.

There is something about the night
that makes your mask,
no matter how tightly fastened
to your soul,
melt under the lava of truth
that sprouts forth
from your deepest heartaches.

There is something about the night
that transforms your answers
into questions;
your strength
into utter weakness;
your hardened heart
into pliable flesh.

There is something about the night
that magnifies the voice of conscience,
and silences the voice of pride.
That exposes relative truth
as an absolute lie.
That makes the soul face its' immortality
and,
in so doing,
realize
that it is woefully unprepared
for eternity.
That makes the human spirit
ask questions
that the foolish mind
dare not consider.

That reminds the fearful
that death is similar to night,
yet much darker,
yet far more fearsome,
and infinitely final.

There is something about the night
that strips the ego of its' smirk,
and draws from your soul
a pleading cry for help.
That bows the stiff back,
and buckles the stubborn knee.

There is something about the night
that draws the human heart
closer
to the Holy Heart.
That opens the deaf ear
to hear
the truths of God.
That opens the tearful eye
to behold
the face of
The Almighty Living God.

There is something about the night.

* * *

Broken

I feel like God has forsaken me,
but the bible says this cannot be.
How long, O Lord, I daily pray,
will sorrow rule me every day?

My life is in a terrible state;
could it be that I repented too late?
Grace is surely greater than sin,
yet grace doesn't lift this pit I'm in.

My 12th hour has long been past,
what little is left, won't last.
My destiny is in your divine hands;
have I strayed too far from your plan?

I'm so confused and in despair,
please, my Lord, hear my prayer.
You have been faithful all of my life,
and used me to lead many to Christ.

You've led me into battle many times,
and those victories were so divine.
I've seen you do miraculous things,
and learned upon you to always lean.

Our intimacy is more precious than gold;
it is divine elixir to my soul.
I hunger for your spiritual embrace;
one touch from you and my pain is erased.

I failed you when I committed that sin,
and for that cause this hell I'm in.
To whom much is given, much is required,
but, Lord, don't let my hope expire.

I knew much trouble would come from that,
but I was weak and my faith grew slack
But remember, my Lord, I prayed for strength,
and after I failed, I did repent.

My only joy is in serving my Lord,
so please Lord, don't close that door.
If you take that honor and privilege away,
how could I live another day?

Hear me, Lord, for I wait on you,
but hope grows dim and my days are few.
Don't cast me aside as others have done,
and don't turn me over to the evil one.

For so many years I proclaimed your name;
I defended the faith and was never ashamed.
I know I failed by yielding to this flesh,
and now I suffer for failing that test.

Satan and his minions gloat over me;
from my fierce assaults they now feel free.
Let not my enemies celebrate my fall,
but lift me up that I again stand tall.

Without your blessings, I daily wonder:
should I end my life, is what I ponder.
I'd hate to leave the world this way,
but in this misery I cannot stay.

I plead with you to deliver me, Lord,
as you have many times before.
I love you with all of my soul and heart,
so please grant me a new start.

*　　*　　*

To Whom Much is Given...

There is a man, whom I once admired,
that fell from an anointed place.
He preached the gospel with fervent fire,
but secretly did things that brought disgrace.

I made the mistake that many of us do,
when I thought he stood above all.
His secret struggles we never knew,
until his enemies plotted his shameful fall.

He spoke the truth and taught morality
to a world in love with sin.
He spoke of judgment as a grim reality,
but forgot that with saints judgment begins.

His love for Christ appeared so strong,
and his commitment crystal clear.
For sure, he knew his passions were wrong,
but pride weakened his Godly fear.

Despite his anointing and gifted teaching,
the man made a grievous mistake.
Holiness preempts passionate preaching,
and the sins of the flesh we must forsake.

There are many who are equally guilty,
yet remain in the pulpit touting truths.
Outside they are clean, but inwardly filthy,
with lives that bear no eternal fruit.

"To whom much is given, much is required,"
is the sobering truth that Jesus proclaimed.
We must daily deny our carnal desires,
or else the Lord will expose our shame.

*   *   *

More Than A Friend

My soul is profoundly depressed,
and my countenance hangs low.
I must find a haven to rest,
a comforting place to go.

My tears pour out like a fountain,
and my heart is torn asunder.
My burdens weigh like a mountain,
and my emotions echo thunder.

Yet, deep within I hear a voice,
speaking softly to my need.
He tells me that I have a choice,
if I merely bow my knee.

He reminds me that I have a friend
living deep within my heart.
An awesome being with power to amend,
whose faithfulness will never depart.

This awesome being is The Great I AM,
and is revealed through His Holy One.
His name is Jesus who's more than a friend;
He is God's only begotten son.

With a peace in my soul, I close my eyes,
and whisper to my God-Friend.
And from deep inside I suddenly realize,
the pain in my soul has come to an end.

* * *

Bad Habits

They're innocently conceived,
but then blossom into sin.
They seduce our thoughts,
and corrupt us from within.

We play with them as children,
not realizing the harm.
We nurture them as teenagers,
enchanted by forbidden charm.

The twenties go and the thirties come,
and our minds can lie no more.
The telltale warnings we failed to heed,
we can no longer ignore.

In brokenness we consider our lives,
and the painful cost of indulgence.
The reckless living, despicable appetites,
and foolish rejection of abstinence.

For so long we defiantly gave in
to habits we thought were cool.
But if we saw through wisdom's eyes,
we'd realize that we were fools.

Now that we've come to our battered end,
we're more willing to concede.
The battle is too great for will alone;
we need Jesus in order to succeed.

By His Grace we've lived this long,
despite our suffering and pain.
He pleads with us to forsake bad habits,
and by faith call on His Name.

*   *   *

Again Will I Stand

Sometimes I fail you so miserably,
and shame and guilt overcomes me.
I desire to know You intimately,
and daily walk in victory.

This wretched flesh seeks its' own will,
and grieves your Spirit dwelling within.
I must yield to your Spirit and be still,
for only then will I conquer sin.

When, like the prodigal, I seek my own way,
I always end up in a dark place.
I quickly repent and urgently pray,
and my contrite heart receives your grace.

You search my heart and reveal my sin,
as I lie prostrate before your throne.
I must confess for cleansing to begin,
then walk in the power of Christ alone.

Although I may fall, again will I stand,
and conquer the trials that await me.
You're faithful to complete what you began
that I might fulfill my destiny.

As I sojourn in this world of decadence,
may I always be mindful of your grace.
May my life bear fruits of repentance,
and may my reward be to see your face.

*   *   *

Trials For Gain

I long to go to that faraway place
where God and His angels dwell.
I want to kiss the Glorious face
of the One who saved me from hell.

As I journey through this world of darkness,
my faith is essential to me.
But in this world there's so much madness,
that from this world I want to flee.

This desire is selfish, I must confess,
but I'm weary of all the trials.
I strive to press on, but need a rest
from all the temptations and self-denials.

I know that the trials serve His purpose,
and perfect my faith and patience.
But when distractions weaken my focus,
my flesh succumbs to indulgence.

Being a Christian is difficult indeed,
for the thing that I would not, I do.
I know by faith that I'm Abraham's seed,
for the bible declares this to be true.

At times I try so hard on my own,
not leaning on the arm of Christ.
The struggles are too hard to bear alone,
but in my weakness He perfects His might.

So I welcome the trials sent for my gain,
and will persevere until the day I die.
God promises an end to all sorrows and pain,
when I go to my home beyond the sky.

* * *

The Rainbow of Christ

Cry out, O my soul,
cry "Abba Father!"
This heart's grown cold;
drift no further.

His Throne awaits
your presence, indeed.
Do not hesitate;
unto Christ cleave.

He hears your cry,
so lift up your voice.
In His rest abide,
and He will bless your choice.

The battle's intense;
the way not clear.
Confess and repent,
and give Christ your fear.

Satan causes strife,
but flees from God's Word.
It's the flesh's appetites,
that you must learn to curb.

God knows your sins,
but much more your sorrow.
He anoints you again,
giving hope for tomorrow.

Remember the victories
God achieved through your hands.
He is God Almighty,
in whose favor you stand.

Yes, you are weary,
and grow tire of the fight.
When the storm is most dreary,
'tis clearer the rainbow of Christ.

*   *   *

Don't Send Me An Angel

Got another tear,
Lord,
that needs wiping away.
Another pain
throbbing
for your touch.
Another wound
aching
for your balm.
Another sorrow
seeking
your joy.
Another disappointment
yearning
for the blessed hope.

Don't send me an angel,
Lord,
with strength in his wings
and soothing words upon his lips.

Got another lonely night,
Lord,
awaiting your presence.
Another shattered dream
that needs resurrecting.
Another crack
in my heart,
gasping
for your Holy seal.

Another tortured memory
squinting
for a glimpse of heaven.
Another pang of guilt
thirsty
for your cleansing blood.

Don't send me an angel,
Lord,
with strength in his wings
and soothing words upon his lips.

Got another mountain to climb,
Lord,
whose peak soars higher than my reach.
I need the wings of an eagle
to ascend.
I got another cross,
Lord,
much heavier than my strength.
I need the strength
of the Lion of Judah.

Got another dark valley,
Lord,
beckoning me
deeper
into its blackness.
I need the Pillar of Fire
to lighten my way.

Been forsaken and betrayed,
Lord.
Please send the Friend
that is closer than a brother.

**Send me You,
Jesus,
Send me You.**

*   *   *

Saved But Not Content

"Well done, good and faithful servant."
are the words I long to hear.
Confessing Christ with a heart repentant
is how God draws me near.

Through Grace beyond understanding,
God chose to rescue me.
He began a process of refining,
preparing me for eternity.

I marvel that I no longer desire
the things that held me fast.
The city of God is where I aspire,
and winning the crown that lasts.

I take no credit for this change
that radically transforms my life.
Glory belongs to that wondrous name
of my Lord and Savior Jesus Christ.

But I am not content with my own salvation,
and my spirit is burdened with sorrow.
So many souls are racing to damnation,
blinded by Satan to their Christ-less tomorrow.

The path they walk, I too once tread,
dancing like fools at hell's gates.
Beyond those doors moan the living dead,
tormented by their eternal fate.

Knowing this how dare I be silent,
or let fear paralyze my tongue.
Though opposed by demons evil and violent,
I'll fight for souls until my life is done.

*   *   *

Even Though, Yet, I Know

Even though now,
stormy waves violently assert themselves against my weakness;
Even though now,
fierce winds tear mercilessly at my naked skin;
Even though now,
my soul, not finding rest, withers up within me;
Even though now,
my tears cease only when my weariness
succumbs to nightmarish slumber;
Even though now,
my world is ravaged by hideous shadows
unleashed from the depths of darkness;
Even though now,
my stricken life whispers "Welcome" to the mocking angel of death.

Yet I Know

The hour is near,
when, at His word, the stormy waves shall be
as a calm lake upon which I walk;
The hour is near,
when He shall cause the fierce winds to be
as a gentle breeze caressing me;
The hour is near,
when He shall cause my soul to sprout wings
and soar with my angels in the sky.
The hour is near,
when His touch shall cause each shed tear to
transform into fountains of living water;
The hour is near,
when the hideous shadows of darkness shall
fearfully flee from the Glory of my Lord..
The hour is near,
when the spirit of my life, standing upon a white
cloud, shall shout praises to His Name
into the wide open expanse of heaven and earth.

*　　*　　*

I Am Weary

I am weary of many things,
but sin tops the list.
Behold how evil hearts sing,
and praise rampant wickedness.

Thieves grow bolder by the hour,
and murderers lust for blood.
The ruthless flaunt destructive power,
and the weak drown in the flood.

Few infants survive full-term
in the war-zone of the womb.
Choice has become a deadly germ,
making the uterus a living tomb.

Husbands and wives go their own way,
mocking the God that made them one.
Their rebellious children go astray,
searching for love but finding none.

Shame and modesty have been displaced
by man's voracious lust for sin.
Acts that once brought disgrace
ignore a conscience dying within.

The hated voice of the righteous one
is scarcely ever heard.
But when the appointed time has come,
God speaks the final word.

My hope is not in this sinful world,
nor do I put my trust in man.
I await the seed of a virgin girl
who holds eternity in His Hand.

*   *   *

Untitled

In this wicked place,
so full of disgrace,
smiles disappear
from every face.

Spirits gather,
venomous their chatter.
From the light
their children scatter.

The end nears,
the scoffers jeer.
But behind their pride,
hearts tremble in fear.

In the barren lands
Satan plans,
the final deception
of reprobate man.

A quiet voice
whispers a choice;
"Embrace my Cross
while my blood is moist."

Who takes heed
to the virgin's seed?
Salvation flows
through wounds that bleed.

Behold the sky,
the signs don't lie.
Listen to the wind,
hear creation's cry.

Fools wail
as judgment hails.
Naked they stand,
at the gates of hell.

In my redeemed soul,
His grace unfolds.
My name is writ
upon a blood-stained scroll.

Sin's penalty
has been removed from me.
A life eternal
is my destiny.

A city of gold
awaits this soul.
Come share with me
divine riches untold.

Find refuge today,
upon your knees do pray:
In my hear, Lord Jesus,
I bid thee to stay.

*   *   *

Only By His Blood

There is a dark place in the human heart,
at the very core of the soul.
In this place evil thoughts germinate,
creating passions way out of control.

It is the heart of imperfection,
the deadly throne room of sin.
We delude ourselves into thinking
we can control this evil within.

The dark and murky place
is the womb that nurtures evil.
It's congenital and not environmental,
and can't be blamed on the devil.

Some trust in reason and morality
to overcome this sin inside.
Satan applauds such foolish thinking,
for he thrives where lies abide.

Others trust in the emotion of love
to conquer our instinct to hate.
But human love is imperfect love,
born from a heart that is reprobate.

We foolishly measure our greatness
by our lofty technical progress.
But behold the evil and debauchery
that causes global distress.

We've subdued so much of our world,
that we think that gods we'll become.
Yet listen to our trifle conversations;
who can control the tongue?

Like actors we play our hypocritical roles,
and dazzle each other with our smiles.
We wear fancy clothes, say the right words,
and deceive each other all the while.

The human heart is evil by nature;
our thoughts prove this to be.
A child must be taught to do what is right,
but on his own will sin naturally.

Surrender to Jesus, The Son of God,
who shed His blood to atone for our sin.
If we repent and trust in Christ,
His blood will cleanse the evil within.

*   *   *

Struggles Before Glory

Feels like I'm spiraling downward,
trapped in a sinking quagmire.
Instead of soaring heavenward,
my flesh pursues its' desire.

Sin got me the scary role
in a Twilight Zone nightmare.
Specters of darkness covet my soul,
enticing me to embrace despair.

I find no joy in this wretched life,
though my smile may seem real.
Over my head hovers clouds of strife,
leaving me numb and unable to feel.

I forsook my thoughts of suicide;
can't leave here that way.
Still, I secretly wish to die,
but He commands me to stay.

I was told that being a Christian
is a difficult life indeed.
I found this true and choose to listen
to Him who died for me.

I naively thought that God would prevent
and evil from touching me.
But He allows the heart that truly repents
to be tried by evil entities.

My Lord is faithful to secure
the rescue of His saints.
To reign with Him I must endure,
and keep the flesh under restraint.

Satan is quite a dreadful foe,
and relentless in his attacks.
But our flesh is the greater woe,
especially when the will is slack.

"Submit to God, resist the devil,
and he must flee from you."
But the flesh presents a greater evil,
by indulging the sin it wants to do.

The flesh is the enemy living within,
while Satan attacks from outside.
The only way for the saint to win
is in the Spirit to always abide.

This truth is easy to grasp,
yet I find it hard to master.
"Lead me Lord" I daily ask,
but my own flesh invites disaster.

I'm entirely frustrated living this way,
and just about ready to concede.
I hunger for that glorious day,
when the flesh will no longer impede.

But until that trumpet sound is heard,
I must deal with this wretched life.
I must do more than just hear the Word;
I must obey it and follow Christ.

Tell me, brother, do we struggle the same,
or have you mastered self-denial?
Take my hand and in Jesus' Name
pray we both overcome our trials.

*   *   *

The Last Days,
The Rapture,
The Apocalypse,
The Second Coming,
The Judgments,
And
Heaven and Hell

Tick-Tock

Sea of faces, going no places;
people gone hysterical.
Satan's pacing, hell is panting;
demons faking miracles.

Birth control, aborted souls;
so many infants die.
Scalpels bleeding, fetuses screaming;
only their angels cry.

Families breaking, so much hating;
why's that baby lame?
Papa-No-Where, Mama-Don't-Care
done fed that baby some pain.

Spouses cheating, both are leaving;
lawyers are getting paid.
Vows mean nothing, they just bluffing;
divorce is having a heyday.

Kids lusting, condoms busting;
AIDS is in the air.
Kids ruling, war-zone schooling;
young ones caught in Satan's snare.

Gangstas wilding, citizens hiding;
wake up Elliot Ness!
Jamaican smoke, Colombian dope;
Mexico's brewing a drug-fest.

Guns blazing, cops misbehaving;
godfather still getting rich.
Gangs playing drive-by slaying;
bodies piling in Satan's pit.

Sugar-coated males, macho females;
gays done got their way.
Morals changing, liberals maiming;
tick-tock to judgment day.

Judges pimping, justice limping;
City Hall for sale.
Candidates posing, their hearts frozen;
forked-tongues hissing fairy-tales.

Churches empty, scandals plenty;
who's minding the sheep?
Greedy preachers, faithless teachers;
shepherds frolicking between the sheets.

Rome's reviving, China's biding;
White House say "bye-bye."
Global merging, New Age surging;
New World Order say "Hi!"

Nature's freaky, weather's creepy;
weatherman's gone viral.
God's fed-up, He's filled His cup;
world's in a hellish spiral.

Israel's nervous, Islam's furious;
blow ye the trumpet in Zion.
They blame the Jews, God's chosen few;
Christ got a rod of iron.

Armies marching, countdown starting;
Armageddon is near.
Behold God's Son, The Risen One;
Satan trembles in fear.

Tick-tock, tick-tock,
seconds left on the clock.
Tick-tock, tick-tock,
the world's about to be shocked.

Tick-tock, tick-tock,
tick

*   *   *

America, Remember God

America, America O land once beautiful,
how sinful have you become.
God blessed you to be most bountiful,
yet His Face you now shun.

Countless people from foreign lands
planted their dreams in your soil.
Your path to glory was paved by God's Hand,
but your wealth has left you spoiled.

God and His ways you blatantly reject,
and persecute those who love Him.
You travel the road of spiritual neglect,
and for this cause your glory dims.

Recall to memory the stories of old
of nations that dared to mock God.
Their prideful ways were evil and bold,
but they were humbled by His iron rod.

One nation is exalted, another stuck-down,
but each destiny is ordained from above.
God is the One who gave you your crown,
yet you deny Him worship and love.

The Lord is merciful beyond all measure,
and His anger is slow to rise.
The death of the wicked gives Him no pleasure,
but mocking Him assures your demise.

The troubles that plague your massive cities,
are merely symptoms of a greater disease.
Examine your ways, behold the atrocities,
and know that in you, God is not pleased.

The men and women leading your government
enact laws that pervert God's truth.
Your school leaders lack moral discernment,
and their ideas corrupt your youth.

Honor for God is forbidden in schools,
while New Age teachings are embraced.
This wickedness produces educated fools,
and hastens the withdrawal of God's Grace.

Your families wither from lack of support,
and a shift to alternative life-styles.
What God joined together is torn by the courts
that are deceived by Satanic guile.

You change your laws to appease the gays,
despite their sin-filled desires.
Remember Sodom and Gomorrah in the old days
whose wickedness God judged by fire.

You murder children helpless in the womb,
spilling their blood for selfish gain.
God hears their cries ascending from their tombs,
and will judge those who caused their pain.

You mete out justice according to wealth,
    and let hardened criminals go free.
Your judicial system is in dire health,
    and often treats victims like enemies.

Media moguls fill airwaves with vice,
    igniting desires way-out-of-control.
They find no profit in producing what's right,
    but whatever is profane they gladly extol.

Pastors and priests speak their own minds,
    and reject the Word of the Lord.
They create fools after their own design,
    who'll follow them through hell's doors.

America, America, land that I once loved,
    examine your ways and repent.
There's a Holy God watching from above,
    and His patience and mercy are nearly spent.

*   *   *

Harbingers

Cataclysmic events occur worldwide,
as the world races through time.
In the sea, earth and beyond the sky,
God's cup of judgment pours out its wine.

The ancient Mayans and the prophets of old,
speak to us from their dusty tombs.
Their words of warning long ago foretold
of global destruction, chaos and gloom.

Tons of fish lie dead in the sand,
then two days later they disappear.
Eruptions in nature baffles man,
and incites in him a supernatural fear.

Birds fall dead while soaring in flight,
and the land creatures share their fate.
These bizarre deaths are a fearsome sight,
yet their sinful ways men won't forsake.

Ominous signs in the sun and moon
baffle the world's scientific minds.
These harbingers warn of coming doom,
created by man's sinful decline.

Trumpet-like sounds fill the skies,
warning of judgments to come.
In awe men listen, but few realize
that the trumpets herald the return of The Son.

UFOs are seen everywhere,
but aren't what they appear to be.
Mankind thinks that ET cares,
but ET is really a demonic entity.

ET pretends he's mankind's creator,
and fools believe this lie.
ET is the supreme masquerader,
and those he deceives will twice die.

Bodies of water suddenly dry up,
and sink-holes dot the land.
Man's sins overflow judgment's cup,
and now in judgment must he stand.

In the Ice lands the weather burns hot,
while the scorching deserts turn icy cold.
What it once was, it now is not,
as even the weather speaks eerily bold.

Earthquakes today, tsunamis tomorrow;
floods and fires everywhere.
Daily nature shouts her mournful sorrow,
but mankind merely covers it's ears.

Woe, woe, woe is what nature speaks
to a people who have gone way too far.
Still, mankind refuses to repent and seek
The One who is called The Morning Star.

Therefore, judgment has been pronounced
against a world that rebels against God.
The laws of God have mankind renounced,
and thereby beckons His Iron Rod.

Now hear me well people of earth,
and incline your ear to wisdom.
What is coming is far, far worse,
so prepare yourselves for God's Kingdom.

Call on Jesus while there is still time,
and repent from your evil ways.
The Lord's heart is infinitely kind,
and He draws near to the one who prays.

*   *   *

A Voice for a Silent People

I feel the pain of a people
who scream in silence.
Their mutilated bodies
bear scars of violence.

They wither in pain,
cries piercing the air.
Though millions are slain,
the world doesn't care.

Sacrificed on altars
their parents have made.
En masse they're slaughtered
by Roe v. Wade.

They're a people too weak
to fight and defend.
They need advocates to speak,
loving hearts to amend.

I arise from my knees
and consider my role.
My courage they need;
my voice strong and bold.

I remember my people
during the horror of slavery.
The abolitionists too few
in a vacuum of bravery.

I consider The Christ
to whom I bow.
I remember His Might,
and find the answer to "How?"

*   *   *

The Warlock's Lament

He died a young man, only thirty-six,
with so much blood on his hands.
His years went by so very quick,
much faster than he planned.

Never one to complain too much,
for his was a life of pleasure.
Wits, greed and a warlock's touch
filled his vaults with blood-stained treasures.

So many women shared his flesh,
but none shared his heart.
He was convinced that he was the best,
and relished playing the part.

No humble pie he ever ate,
no goal he failed to achieve.
Destiny, he thought, was his to create,
a satanic lie meant to deceive.

In his mind he stood above all,
like a king perched atop a throne.
He heard, but rejected, the Lord's call,
bidding God to leave him alone.

Such a foolish man not to realize
that God is the source of life.
Sin and pride blinded his eyes
to the sovereignty of Jesus Christ.

Jesus, he thought, was a misguided man,
who wasted his time on the weak.
"All that power in a carpenter's hand;
he should crush his foes, not lift the meek."

He set his heart against the Lord,
and blasphemed His Holy name.
Proudly he raced through that door
that leads to death and eternal pain.

He joined forces with the Lord's foes,
and was cursed with a reprobate mind.
Then his life became a litany of woes,
cut-off forever from Glory Divine.

He served Satan well without restraint,
pursuing the coveted crown.
He warred against the Lord's holy saints,
enraged that none were hell-bound.

But Satan he knew not so well,
for he thought he'd share Satan's throne.
Indeed, a crown awaited him in hell,
a crown of fire and brimstone.

Though dead inside, he yet did care
for one he hid from his world.
Her father's eyes and golden hair,
hinted that she was his little girl.

He poured his heart into her life,
and shielded her from his evil ways.
But Satan demanded her sacrifice,
before the end of her innocent days.

For the very first time he refused to obey,
knowing too well the horrible cost.
He offered instead others to slay,
saints not counted among the lost.
Satan laughed at the warlock's love,
and demanded "Sacrifice her to me."
With desperate eyes searching heaven above,
the warlock uttered an urgent plea:

"If truly you are God's merciful Son,
grant my one and only desire.
My precious daughter is yet so young,
save her soul from the lake of fire."

Soon thereafter, a messenger was sent,
and the girl received God's Grace.
But the warlock believed he could not repent,
and his own sins could not be erased.

Hearing his own pleading to Christ,
enraged Satan's heart of hate.
"Father and daughter will I sacrifice,
and drag their souls through hell's gates."

Satan himself executed the pair;
the flames in the car hissed his name.
The warlock's soul screamed in fear
at the sight of hell's chambers of pain.

The veil was lifted between the two worlds,
as demons fled from The Glorious One.
No Satan or demon dared approach the girl,
who was held in the arms of God's Holy Son.

In hell below she heard the warlock wail,
and her last tears for him she shed.
For a moment she peered into the depths of hell,
and saw her father among the burning dead.

"Lord, she pleaded, is it yet too late
to rescue his soul from the fire?"
Jesus replied "He chose to forsake
the gift of God for the father of liars.

Had he received my saving hand,
he would be with us in paradise.
But he rejected God's salvation plan,
and mocked my atoning sacrifice.

His choice came with a terrible price
that none can afford to pay.
For this reason I gave my life,
because I AM the only way.

Behold, my beloved, your place of rest,
the golden city prepared for my own.
Now lay your head upon my chest,
and bask in the glory of your eternal home."

For a moment the Lord let the warlock see
his daughter soaring to heaven above.
With tears in His eyes, Jesus looked at his enemy,
and whispered "For you too I shed my blood."

*   *   *

Voices Of Angels

I speak words,
sounding strange to myself.
I feel feelings
piercing deep within myself.
I see visions of skeletons
drowning in tears.
I dream dreams of nations
crumbling in fear.

**Voices of angels
speaking as one.
Receive the Christ,
God's Anointed Son.**

The heart of humanity
pulsates with gloom.
Behind arrogant faces,
hide souls of doom.
Weep over the children
whose ways have gone bad.
Their violence and hatred
makes tomorrow sad.
The men and women
change their roles.
The strong become weak,
and the weak grow bold.

**Voices of angels
speaking as one.
Receive the Christ,
God's Anointed Son.**

Satan and his minions
have conspired a plan,
to dethrone the Christ,
and rule over man.
His method is to blind
the searching eye of the soul.
He imitates God,
and entices men with gold.
We quickly approach the final chapter.
Come out of the darkness,
and prepare for the rapture.

*   *   *

The Rapture and Beyond

The archangel shouted and the trumpet sounded,
but the scoffers were left behind.
As the saints soared the scoffers were astounded,
regretting the chance they declined.

The clouds parted and our Lord appeared,
surrounded by His heavenly hosts.
The earth trembled and the scoffers feared,
as our bodies were changed by the Holy Ghost.

The dead arose first, then the living were changed,
all in the twinkling of an eye.
The Lord returned for His own to claim,
and be re-united with His bride in the sky.

This is the day that the scriptures declared,
and God The Father is ready.
The angels attend and the bride is prepared,
for the Bridegroom's glorious wedding.

After seven years our Lord will return,
and with the saints He will rule on earth.
Then after a thousand years this earth will burn,
destroying forever the remnant of the curse.

Then the darkest day in all of eternity
finally dawns upon man.
Those who rejected the Son of Divinity
will now in His judgment stand.

Woe to the one whose name is not found
in the Lamb's Book of Life.
In the lake of fire his soul will be bound
for rejecting the Lord Jesus Christ.

*   *   *

New Age America

Silver tears fall from an evil sky
as a poor boy,
chasing dreams much faster than himself,
plays hide and seek
with bullets blazing his name.
A once-pretty woman watches from the gateway,
until a stranger pays their way back to hell.
An old man wearing a face
sculpted by worse-than-hard-times,
clenches his bottle.
On a distant planet
The God-Man
hears the old man's silent lament.
"O sweet Jesus, why did you die for me?"

A giddy couple,
lost in the ecstasy of new love,
forget their place in time and space.
Their ecstatic odyssey
hurls them beyond the borders of their world
and into the realm of the lost
and not found.
The night creatures salivate;
soon their feast begins.
A fatherless child quivers in fear.
Her body screams,
but spine-chilling fear seals her lips.
Mommy's pharmacist
brutally finds his payment
between her five year old thighs.

Legal ones draped in black robes
perch atop thrones of justice.
Their judgments echo
the voice of the highest bidder.
Their souls vomit justice.
Their consciences speak no more.
But a fearful trembling,
divinely engineered into their souls,
reminds them of a Great White Throne
awaiting them just beyond their last breath.
There will be no echoes.

Men desire the flesh of their own kind,
and women their kind.
They vacate their hidden closets
and shove morality in.
Satan and their wealth convinces the lawmakers
that their abomination
is a gay alternative.
Down below,
hell snickers.

Husbands and wives
proclaim their empty vows
unto each other.
They wed in grand fashion,
then trivialize and forsake the marriage that follows.

Satan dances victoriously
over the decomposing corpse
of yet another family.
He boasts,

"Give me one generation of fatherless families
and I will rule the land."
Up yonder,
The Sovereign One
seethes.

An innocent people,
yet born,
are sacrificed on the altar of Roe v. Wade.
Golden scalpels spill their blood.
Scientists and the sophisticated ones
applaud the rejuvenating propensity
of fetal tissue.
Mothers and fathers
hail the virtues of choice.
And in the midst of the applause and the hails,
tiny innocent souls,
screeching in agony,
learn to die
before learning to live.
Wombs,
their cradles of life,
transform into chambers of torture.
Placentas,
their life-giving life-lines,
transform into life-suffocating nooses.
Surgical trash cans
become their final resting place.

But the One who created them
and calls them by name,
receives their tortured souls unto Himself.
He becomes their Father and Mother.
He wipes away their tears,
silences their spine-chilling screams,

and gives them new and perfect bodies.
The angels become their teachers and playmates.
Paradise
is their very own playground.
Then,
with fire in His eyes,
God awaits their unrepentant executioners.

Hollywood and Madison Ave.
inject their philosophies
and assorted pervert-ologies
into the fertile minds of soon-to-be-fools.
Their young bodies become crap tables.
AIDS-roulette is their game of choice.
Tragically they discover,
so dreadfully too late,
that sin rolls deadly dice.

Demons,
masquerading as gods,
hiss seductive melodies through their fiery flutes.
Their serpentine priests
slither in rhythm to the hypnotic sounds.
Channeling their ascended masters,
they chant with one voice,
blinding the vacant eyes,
tickling the deaf ears,
and lulling mesmerized souls into damnation.

They convince themselves
that their kingdom is at hand.
They convince themselves
that evolution has catapulted them into godhood.
Yet,
their ascended masters still tremble

at the Name of Jesus,
and the priests remain captive
in the grip of the grave.
Hell awaits them with open jaws,
and fiery claws.

America, America,
you no longer bow at the altar of
The Sovereign,
Almighty Living God.

The world watches as the American dream
mutates
into a hellish nightmare.
America now treads upon that highway,
that broad-way,
that leads to destruction.

Down below,
Hell laughs.

*   *   *

In The Twinkling of An Eye

It began ever so slightly,
barely audible;
a decibel below a whisper.
A curious sound,
more felt than heard.
A visceral reaction;
a cellular tingling.

Then silence.
Moments pass.

A second sound,
trumpet like.
Piercing.
Commanding.
Omnipresent.
Extraterrestrial!

My rapt attention
is no mere act of will;
it is compelled.
A peculiar light,
shimmering and brilliant,
emanates from my brown skin.
The tone of my skin color,
and the hue of the peculiar light
blend
into a golden aura.

My muscles twitch,
reshape,
then expand
radically but not painfully.
Internal organs
change.
Some disappear.
New ones emerge.
My body pulsates
with a new and awesome
power.
I instinctively know
my transformed body is
invincible and immortal!!

My old body
now
appears to be no more
than twenty-five years old!

My heart,
once filled with life-sustaining blood,
now pumps
an eternal-life-sustaining elixir.
My visual acuity
penetrates the clouds,
the skies,
and even the heavens.

Behold!
The third heaven,
The Planet of God,
is in clear view.

Then silence.
A moment passes.

A third sound,
a prolonged trumpet blast,
is accompanied by
a mighty rushing wind.
Just beyond the clouds
hovers
a powerful archangel,
majestic and brilliant in appearance,
blowing his golden shofar.
Gabriel!

The blast of the shofar
shatters the sound barrier.
My clothes
drop
from my new celestial body.
A brilliant white robe,
embroidered
in heaven's gold,
without spot nor wrinkle,
spontaneously wraps itself
around my new body.

Suddenly
I begin to ascend,
slowly at first,
then as fast as the twinkling of an eye.
The earth recedes,
and dark clouds,
darker than pitch black,
envelope the staggering planet.
I see
what appears to be
millions of brilliant stars
ascending with me
from the four corners of earth;
summoned,
as I,
by Gabriel's golden shofar.

Then,
above the clouds,
above Gabriel with his golden shofar,
Stands One,
whose Majesty and Glory
dims the sun and the heavens.
Even they bow!
The shofar falls silent.
Gabriel
hovers in reverential awe and wonder.
His dazzling wings spread out in ecstatic praise.
Innumerable angels,
breathtakingly beautiful to behold,
gaze upon this Most Exalted One.

With outstretched arms,
This Glorious One,
This God-Man,
Jesus,
beckons the ascending stars;
He beckons me!

Lo!
In the palms of His outstretched hands,
I see the wounds
that were pierced by my sins.
All about Him
the ascending stars gather,
escorted by divine beings.
I realize that
I, too,
am flanked
by the most beautiful,
most powerful,
celestial beings ever seen by redeemed souls.

Suddenly,
a heavenly choir appears.
The song they sing,
and the heavenly music that fills the universe,
announce
The Bridegroom.

The redeemed bride
gazes in holy awe
upon her betrothed,
her Savior,
her God.

At the Summit of all creation,
on the Planet of God,
The Father
rises
from His Celestial Throne.
His Train
fills the universe.
Glorious angels
which cannot be numbered,
bow
in His Presence.
God The Father
announces to the universe
the wedding of
His Son,
The Lamb of God.

*   *   *

The Four Horsemen of The Apocalypse

The colors of the horses galloping from hell
are white, red, black and pale.
The means by which they snatch man's breath
are peace, war, famine and death.

The rider on the white horse has a bow;
through peace he causes blood to flow.
The rider on the red horse has a sword,
and he slays millions through global war.

The rider on the black horse holds two scales,
and by way of famine he prevails.
Death is the rider atop the pale one,
and hell follows when Death is done.

The white horse ushers in the Tribulation,
a seven year period of global devastation.
A world ruler being full of blasphemy
rises to become God's chief enemy.

The people of the world will worship this man,
whose power comes from his father Satan.
He causes all men to receive his mark,
except those who have Christ in their heart.

No human or angel can take his life;
he fears no one except Jesus Christ.
Of such evil there has never been
as that which indwells this man of sin.

His hate is focused on Abraham's seed,
but the saints and Jews will together cleave.
Many who place their faith in Christ,
will do so at the cost of their life.

From the dead they will rise when Christ returns,
but those with the mark will surely burn.
Satan and his spawn have a singular goal,
to cast into hell myriads of souls.

Asteroids will fall from the darkened sky,
as men vainly seek for places to hide.
The rivers and seas will turn blood red;
humans and creatures will both lie dead.

The sun scorches men with intense heat,
and gruesome sores cover head to feet.
Darkness will blanket the kingdom of the beast;
behold the kings marching from the east.

The Day of God's wrath is finally here;
both man and demon tremble in fear.
The demons in hell are now set free,
and they feast on souls voraciously.

Men will seek death, but death will flee;
still men refuse to bow heart and knee.
The Gospel will be preached as never before,
proclaiming Jesus Christ as the only door.

The world has never seen such awesome fury,
but at the height of despair, behold, Christ's Glory!
The sky rolls back and Christ is revealed,
and on earth He shall enforce His Will.

The battle of Armageddon thus begins;
the nations are led by the man of sin.
Christ and His armies descend from the sky;
one word from Christ and his enemies die.

Into the abyss will Satan be cast;
for a thousand years his confinement will last.
The beast and his prophet come to their end,
when in the lake of fire they both descend.

Christ sends His angels to gather the nations
to stand before Him for the final separation.
The goats on the left and the sheep on the right;
the sheep will be the ones to enter Paradise.

The Kingdom of Christ will then begin;
evil and darkness will not enter in.
For a thousand years Christ will rule;
His enemies have become His footstool.

Prepare even now for the events to come,
by giving your heart to God The Son.
Many on the earth when the horsemen arrive
will receive the mark and twice die.

All who receive the mark of Anti-Christ
will be cut-off forever from eternal life.
Receiving that mark cannot be reversed,
but condemns you to an eternal curse.

Lucifer

Long before the fall of Adam and Eve,
God created an angel of great wisdom.
His beauty and pride led him to believe,
that he could rule God's kingdom.

This angel was perfect in all of his ways,
and preeminent above all.
But pride and greed led him astray,
and was the reason for his infamous fall.

God named him Lucifer, the bearer of light,
and clothed him in precious stones.
God gave him beauty, wisdom and might,
and granted him the honor of guarding God's throne.

He led the worlds in praising The Almighty,
for music came forth from his very soul.
His supremacy was second only to The Trinity,
and because of this he grew bold.

But Lucifer coveted the Glory of the Lord,
and devised a very evil plan.
God gave him much but he wanted more;
in God's place he wanted to stand.

He convinced himself God was too small
to crush his ambitious plan.
His foolish pride only hastened his fall
and earned him the name of Satan.

His evil plan caused his fall from grace,
along with a third of his kind.
In judgment God sent him to a faraway place,
and left him to a reprobate mind.

Satan then devised an alternative plan
in his quest to usurp The Most High.
He decided to corrupt the innocence of man,
and deceived Eve with a blasphemous lie.

In a single stroke his hopes were revived,
as dominion of earth fell into his hands.
He caused man to sin, knowing he'd die,
but the love of God he didn't understand.

God's love is unsearchable and so are His way,
but Satan didn't grasp this at all.
God forgave man and promised one day
a Seed would redeem them from the fall.

Wickedness increased as time passed by,
and Satan thought he had the final word.
But one night in Bethlehem a Holy Baby cried,
the sound of which the angels heard.

This Holy Child who was named Jesus,
is the promised Savior of the world.
This Messiah that God sent us,
was born of Mary, a virgin girl.

He heals the sick, resurrects the dead,
and reveals the Father to you and I.
By His wounds He crushed Satan's head,
and out of love for us He chose to die.

Lucifer began as an angel of light,
filled with divine illumination.
Satan will perish at the hand of Christ,
as foretold in the book of Revelation.

But until he's cast into the lake of fire,
Satan will deceive as many as he can.
Salvation of souls is God's prime desire,
and Satan wants to thwart God's plan.

So beware, my friend, and receive God's Son,
lest you share in Satan's fate.
Open your heart to the Most Holy One,
and do so now before its too late.

*   *   *

Maestro of Death

The maestro of destruction,
master of seduction,
he leads the fallen angels
in a fatal revolution.

A gruesome, hideous sight,
he dons a cloak of light,
in a diabolical scheme
to mimic Jesus Christ.

Through clenched teeth of iron,
he roars like a lion.
He kills the virgin daughters
of the King of Zion.

There is an appointed day,
when Satan will have his way.
Terror will grip the world,
except those who know to pray.

This maestro of death has one desire,
to fill with souls the lake of fire.
His final deception pivots on a man,
an evil son whom Satan will sire.

Over the nations his son will reign,
promising peace but delivering pain.
Many saints will give their lives
for believing in Jesus' Name

As he takes his blasphemous stand,
his wrath will turn on Abraham.
Desperately he tries to abort
the fulfillment of God's Holy plan.

His hellish fury knows no bounds;
eternal damnation is his crown.
He knows that Michael and his angels
are swiftly coming to cast him

Remove the wax from the deaf ear,
and bend the knees in reverent fear.
Behold the signs of this evil time;
the Day of the Lord is drawing near.

*   *   *

Anti-Christ, Son Of Perdition

Another page too quickly turns,
as John's revelation unfolds.
So many souls desperately yearn
to be free of Satan's stranglehold.

Satan spins his evil web
at a fearful, frenzied pace.
This god-father of the living dead
has no time to waste.
His son sits upon the white horse,
holding a bow in his hand.
Behind quasi-peace lurks an evil force,
plotting the damnation of man.

New Age fools worship the beast,
damning themselves with his mark.
Woe to Jacob in yonder east
when Daniel's 70th week starts.

Europe nurtures this lawless one,
who will cause old Rome to rise.
But when his evil work is done,
Europe will share his violent demise.

John Paul rides the beasts' back
to the pinnacle of religious power.
In a jealous rage the beast will attack
and drag John Paul from his scarlet tower.

The beast will receive a mortal wound,
causing his minions to wail.
He rises from his Houdini tomb,
sealing the damned under his spell.

His signs and wonders beguile the fools,
and dazzle the eyes of the blind.
Yet, he himself is only a tool
gearing in motion to God's design.

He's the Abomination of Desolation
that Daniel foretold would be.
His blasphemy reeks of reprobation,
supreme in the annals of infamy.

His wrath rages against the saints,
and the children of father Abraham.
He feasts on them without restraint,
killing to the cheers of the damned.

He is given authority over the nations,
making him the ruler of the world.
His reign will be of seven years duration,
ended by the seed of a virgin girl.

Demonized armies form their alliance,
as they march to the valley of Jehoshaphat.
Against Christ they gather in fatal defiance,
and will drink the brew of God's wrath.
O son of Satan, thou spawn of evil,
behold the end of your macabre life.
You drank the blood of God's holy people,
now taste the vengeance of Jesus Christ.

Millions untold will share his fate
in the river that flows with fire.
Utterly lost, they discover too late
that a soul without Christ will twice expire.

*   *   *

The Unholy Trinity

Master deceiver, vile accuser;
the angel that fell from Grace.
Once divine, his beauty shined,
until he coveted the God's place.

Perfect at birth, now roaming the earth,
seeking souls to devour.
He spawned a son, John revealed this one,
destined to yield global power.

By miracles he deceives those who disbelieve
the sure Word of Jesus Christ.
Four horses he rides, behind peace he hides,
slaughtering millions in his blood-thirsty plight.

He reigns seven years, souls drowning in tears;
his wrath knows no bounds.
The woman in the east flees from the beast;
twelve stars she wears as a crown.

The saints he'll behead to the cheers of the dead,
but they will rise to rule for a thousand years.
Many will believe the two olive trees,
who make the anti-Christ tremble in fear.

His prophet shall arise, drawing fire from the sky,
causing all to worship the beast.
This unholy trinity imitates Divinity,
but this evil triune will fall in defeat.

With His armies He'll come, God's risen Son,
at the end of the seven year reign.
The unholy trinity will burn for eternity;
"Jesus is Lord" shall all proclaim.

*   *   *

Armageddon

The winds whirl,
and the clouds scatter.
The sky curls,
and the earth staggers.

The people are scared,
and the creatures disperse.
The land is bare,
and the demons curse.

Their reign they know
has come to and end,
as the trumpets blow,
and Christ descends.

The armies from the east,
and the best from the west
are prepared for a feast,
blinded by their quest.

The valley of Jehoshaphat
moves to center stage.
Fools beckon God's wrath;
none survive His rage.

The stars move aside,
and heaven is revealed.
Saints and angels side by side,
as Christ descends on the hill.

The armies grow weak,
as they march high-stepping.
Their courage grows bleak,
as they face Armageddon.

The Lord of the saints
speaks His Word.
His enemies fall faint,
as the war cries are heard.

The fowls of the air
circle the valley.
Feast time is here,
many bodies to tally.

The beast who would rule
no longer stands.
His reign so cruel,
now crushed by the God-Man.

The way is clear,
and the earth is new.
Christs' Kingdom is here
for me and for you.

Peace will reign
for a thousand years.
Yet once again
from the beast we'll hear.

For a season he'll prey
to reveal his descendants.
Then in the lake he'll stay,
with the unrepentant.

The old earth will pass away,
and the heavens will go.
With Christ we will stay,
and His Kingdom will grow.

*   *   *

Hell

Far underground
where darkness abounds;
none escape from this prison.
Created for the devil,
enlarged for lost people;
the cost for their fatal decision.

Engulfed in flames,
Hell is its name;
woe unto all who enter its' doors.
Horrific torments
for Hell's residents,
because they rejected the Lord.

Hell is not rehab
for souls gone bad;
but a place designed for punishment.
Souls grow worse
as they burn in the earth,
and forever they remain unrepentant.

No preacher's rendition
can capture the conditions
of this macabre abode of the damned.
A fearsome sight
is their gruesome plight;
far beyond the scope of man.

Fear everywhere,
souls in despair;
no more hope for the lost.
In life they disobeyed,
and refused to pray
to Christ who died on the Cross.

No more rest
for souls who cared less
for God's holy Word.
They chose this place
by scorning God's Grace,
and rejecting the truths they heard.

Water nowhere
and worms everywhere,
feeding on the souls trapped therein.
Full of decadence
and void of repentance,
in Hell they pay for their sins.

Remorseful souls
bearing sins manifold;
twice the lost taste death.
They mocked the Christ,
and His sacrifice;
the lake of fire is all that's left.

No love in Hell,
no peace as well;
only excruciating pain.
Beyond Hell's gates,
it's way too late
to call upon Jesus' Name.

Souls yearn to warn
their kin who scorn
the reality of such a horrible place.
They want to return
so others won't burn,
by telling them to receive God's Grace.

The demons rejoice
at the sinner's choice
to live life in their own way.
The demons wait
at death's iron gates,
to torment souls that west astray.

The Lord weeps
when the wicked sleep,
and close their eyes for the last time.
The Lord knows
that eternal woes
await the soul that's blind.

Don't trust in yourself,
or anything else,
for Christ is the only way.
Apart from Christ
there is no life,
only darkness and decay.

In life we must
upon Jesus trust,
in order to enter eternal life.
Open your hearts,
from your sins depart,
and receive God's gift of Jesus Christ.

Do not delay
yet another day,
for tonight may be your last.
Christ is kind
and has a future sublime,
for those who sincerely ask.

*   *   *

Judgment Day
The Great White Throne

It is the darkest day that will ever be,
when the dead stand before God's Throne.
There will be no appeal or amnesty,
and all will stand before God alone.

The great and small will be the same,
so too will the rich and poor.
All will stand alone in their shame,
for having rejected the Risen Lord.

Good works, they thought, would open the gate
to heaven and eternal life.
They believed this lie and discovered too late
that the doorway to Heaven is Jesus Christ.

Many roads were chosen, many faiths believed,
but all of this to no avail.
They bought Satan's lies and were deceived;
a choice that led them straight to hell.

Those who escaped the justice of man,
will now have to pay the cost.
No bribe, wit or powerful hand
will save the soul that's lost.

Every thought, word and sinful act,
Christ will examine on that day.
Their assignment in the lake pivots on this fact,
and is revealed to all who turned away.

Eternal damnation is not God's desire;
this is why Jesus died for us.
Yet many will choose the lake of fire,
for in vain things they put their trust.

Take heed now to God's warning;
I beg you not to delay.
Turn from your foolish scorning,
and on your knees fervently pray:

Heavenly Father, I confess my sins,
and ask that you forgive me.
I believe Jesus died and rose again
that I might live for eternity.

I receive Lord Jesus into my heart,
and bid Him to always remain.
Today, in Christ, my new life starts,
and in me will Jesus eternally reign.

*   *   *

The Bema Seat

He stands no more at the door,
but has now entered in.
Let all rejoice who wait on the Lord,
and prepare to don eternal skin.

Gabriel raises his golden shofar,
as his brothers spread their wings.
The sun, moon and the stars
announce the Coming of the King.

Indeed the wait has been so long,
and the journey hard at times.
But by His Spirit we stood strong,
and like dazzling stars we will shine.

Our sins He'll not remember;
no punishment meted out.
Our motives is what He considers,
and our faithfulness is what He touts.

Gold, silver and precious stones
will survive His test of fire.
He rewards the acts of love we've shown,
for this is the Lord's desire.

All work done out of selfishness,
is straw, hay and wood.
All that's done out of righteousness
is work that God calls good.

In Heaven's bank invest your treasure,
which is far better than worldly gold.
For heavenly wealth shall last forever,
but worldly pursuits will destroy your soul.

So prepare to stand at the Bema Seat
by serving Christ with all your heart.
Our righteous works will stand the heat,
and eternal rewards will Christ impart.

*   *   *

The New Jerusalem

Far above the earth, shining throughout the universe,
The New Jerusalem awaits The Bride.
Jesus is its architect, prepared for His Holy Elect,
forever therein will she reside.

Mansions so divine are heavenly designed;
there's eternal wealth for all.
By God's Grace, He reserved a place
for those He chose before the fall.

Treasures untold await faithful souls,
whose lives were a living sacrifice.
Rewards He will give to the saints who live
as servants of God reflecting His Light.

Crowns of precious stones, we'll lay at His Throne;
for our glory radiates from Him.
The good we've done through God The Son
shouts Glory and Praise to Elohim.

Sorrows no more, boundless joy in store,
and the saints will forever reign.
Streets of gold, saints never grow old;
our glorified bodies will never know pain.

No curse of sin nor darkness therein;
God's Glory is its source of light.
No strife or hate beyond Heaven's gates,
only love and joy for the Bride of Christ.

The gates of pearl, the entrance to that world,
tell the story of The Lord's wounds.
His blood He shed, then He rose from the dead
and is coming back for His bride real soon.

Our guardians through the years, the angels live there,
and make preparations for the royal bride.
They were faithful to serve, not one ever swerved;
throughout the journey they stood at our side.

Angels spread their wings in reverence to The King,
as the saints soar in rapturous flight.
Lift-up your eyes; Jerusalem descends from the sky.
Behold the glorious sight!

*   *   *

Meditations

A heart that does not emit love,
like the womb that does not bring forth a child,
is barren.

*   *   *

Man wanting to be
God,
claiming to be
God,
does not make him
God.
His wanting,
his claiming,
in fact,
makes man less than
the creature.
For even the lowly
creature
knows its place.

*   *   *

For each measure
of immoral indulgence,
double the measure
of spiritual darkness.
Thereafter,
the formula increases exponentially.

*   *   *

The flesh seeks its own desire,
driven by passions of the heart.
If, then, the heart be wicked,
how great the folly of him
who heeds its voice.

*   *   *

Prayers spoken in solitude
and anointed in tears,
resonates the loudest
in the Father's ears.

*   *   *

I observed the child in his innocence,
untouched by the evil in the world.
I observed the natural unfolding of
deceit, selfishness, violence and hatred
in the heart of innocence.
These behaviors manifested without the impetus
of external solicitation or conditioning.
The fruit of sin blooms naturally.
Conversely,
I observed the characteristics of
love, selflessness, peace and honesty
manifesting themselves
only at the behest of sustained external
solicitation and conditioning.
How, then, did we come to believe
that the human heart is basically good?

*   *   *

Guilt to the soul
is as
pain is to the body.
Hearken,
therefore,
to the warning of each.

*   *   *

Bitterness cripples the heart,
but forgiveness restores health.

*   *   *

When one sets one's mind
to do right,
one discovers how much
the heart is inclined,
indeed craves,
to do wrong.

*   *   *

A certain man was employed by a major bank as
an investment broker. He worked at this
bank for several years and earned a high six figure income. He was
married and had three sons ages 13, 15 and 16. His wife and mother
of his children, was a homemaker and relished the role. Despite his
high salary, the man embezzled over a million dollars from the bank.
In due time, the embezzlement was discovered and the man was sent
to jail. Although he was represented by a nationally renowned law
firm, he was convicted and sentenced to fifteen years in prison. The
family's income and style of living was lost due to the man's crime.

The wife, who had no previous work experience, obtained
a full-time position as a receptionist in a government office.
She also took a part-time evening job as a cashier at a local
supermarket. The family had to move out of their semi-palatial
suburban home and into a one bedroom urban apartment.
The sons, who had attended a prestigious private school and were all
stand-out students, were enrolled in an overcrowded urban school. In
time the boys rebelled and became involved with drugs; the youngest
developed a serious drug addiction. The older two boys got into
trouble with the law and were sent to a juvenile detention center.

*   *   *

Was the suffering that the family endured caused by the judge's sentencing of the father, or was it caused by the man's crime? Should we conclude that the judge was insensitive or mean because of the potential and actual detrimental consequences that his sentencing would have on the banker's family? In view of these potential familial hardships, should the judge have pardoned the man?

Likewise, is God responsible for the suffering in the world that results from mankind's sins?

Consider this when you are tempted to ask the question "Why does God allow suffering in the world?"

CH. 6

GOD'S TENACIOUS RESCUE

The Fervency of God's Love

by Lance Watson

It was during the spring in the year 1988. I was employed by a federal agency as a claims adjudicator. My job was to determine the medical eligibility of a person applying for disability benefits; I had been working for this agency for two years. I enjoyed this work because it allowed me to utilize skills and abilities honed over the years. It also afforded me the opportunity to help those in need; the pay and benefits were also good.

One day I received the claim of a young woman named Helen. Helen was thirty-one years old and a social worker was applying on her behalf. Helen was afflicted with the HIV virus and was, in fact, at the end stage of the disease. Helen was homeless and the only contact information we had on her was a post office box and the social worker's name and phone number. We also had an antiquated medical report from a local hospital.

As I began to review the file an unmistakable and powerful feeling swept over me. I immediately knew that God was very interested in this person and, by His Spirit, was alerting me to pay particular and special attention to this claim. I immediately became very interested in the claim as well. Unfortunately, I could not locate Helen and the social worker lost contact with her. The post office box was no longer active in her name. However, the social worker was able to provide me with the telephone number of one of Helen's cousins.

I telephoned the cousin, identified myself and the purpose of my call. The cousin informed me that she did not know Helen's whereabouts and, astonishingly, she added that she did not care where she was. "That b—ch stole from me and she can drop dead for all I care!" Okay, this was clearly a dead end. However, the cousin did provide me with the names and telephone numbers of three other relatives. I thanked her and, after telling me never to contact her again regarding Helen, we hung up. I proceeded to contact the three other relatives. Unbelievably, each of the three relatives I contacted did not want to cooperate and literally hated Helen. It was most disheartening that, despite Helen's terminal condition, none of her relatives wanted to help her even though their cooperation required little to no effort. Why did her relatives hate this terminally ill young woman?

Helen was a crack addict. She stole from everyone and anyone. She was a prostitute and had AIDS. And, perhaps worse of all, Helen had three little children whom she abandoned. Quite honestly, I could understand their disenchantment with Helen; she was a piece of work. The fact that she was a ruthless thief and abandoned three babies would have put me off also. Yet, what I found peculiar was my own reaction to Helen. I had an unmistakable and powerful compassion for the woman even though I did not know her, and what I did know of her would normally put me off. I felt deeply sorry for this woman. This perplexed me until I realized that what I was feeling for Helen, God Himself felt and He allowed me to share His heart for the poor soul.

I gave all of my attention to this claim. But I just could not locate Helen and we had a policy that allowed us only a certain amount of time to locate the claimant. If we could not locate the claimant within the allotted time frame, we had to close out the claim due to "whereabouts unknown." I chose to ignore the policy and continued to work the claim. I knew it was God laying this burden on my heart. Although I was a young Christian, I knew when God placed a burden on your heart for someone or something, one had to work the burden until the Lord Himself released you from it.

However, after a week or so my supervisor questioned me about the status of the claim. I informed him of the particulars. He asked me why I was holding onto the claim despite the claimant's unknown whereabouts. I told him that if I could only locate her, I would be able to approve the claim for benefits. He correctly told me that I did everything possible to locate her and told me to close out the claim. Technically, he was correct; I could not justify holding onto the claim. And now that my supervisor was aware of the particulars, I had no choice but to release the claim. As I began writing my close out report, I silently prayed to the Lord. Surprisingly, I found myself holding back tears as I prayed. I felt such a profound sadness for this lady. Yea, she was a "low-life" and the type of person I normally would have nothing to do with. But she was all alone, hated by everyone and fatally ill. Right there at my desk I pleaded with the Lord to send someone who really knew Him and loved Him to Helen. I said "Lord, you know where she is. I've done all that I could but I have to let go of this claim. Lord, she has no one; she's alone in the world and desperately needs help. I don't think she knows you. Please send her someone to help her. In Jesus name I commit her to you." I completed my close out report and released the claim. I did not understand why God gave me such a burden for the woman knowing that my attempts to contact her would be unsuccessful. I knew that I did everything possible to find the woman but yet I was left with a feeling of guilt. I felt that I let God and Helen down. And I also felt that Satan won. I hated that. My day was ruined.

Fast forward about eight months. The computer assigned all cases and we were never assigned the same case twice. I continued to pray for Helen and committed her to the Lord. Then one day I was assigned the claim of a woman who, like Helen, was 31 and had full blown AIDS. This woman was also represented by a social worker. There were already reports in the file but lacked sufficient information to make a medical determination. This woman was a drug addict, homeless and alone; the similarities between her and Helen were remarkable. I wanted to do for this woman what I failed to do for Helen. Unfortunately, however, I could not locate the claimant. I also felt a strong compassion for this person. Since I could not locate her in the allotted time, I began to write my close out report. As I was writing the close out report, my telephone rang. It was a psychiatric social worker calling from a hospital located in the central portion of the state. After identifying himself, he asked me if I was handling his client's claim. I affirmed that I was but informed him that we could not locate her and that I was completing the close out report as we spoke. Then he informs me that his client was a patient in that hospital. This was good news. I asked him to fax me her medical reports. He agreed to do so and immediately faxed her medical records to me.

The claimant was diagnosed with HIV encephalopathy. This is a condition that is clinically similar to a person with dementia or Alzheimer's disease. The condition leaves the person with essentially no mental functioning; they are clueless. Such a condition will inevitably result in death in a short period of time. The claimant was non-functional, bedridden and completely emaciated. I was able to approve the claim.

Now the claim took on a whole new supernatural dimension. I called the psychiatric social worker, thank him for the reports and informed him that the claim would be approved. Then I asked him (let's call him Joe) if the patient had a telephone in her room. The question just blurted out. I thought it strange that I should ask Joe that because the patient was non-communicable. Surprisingly, Joe said that she did have a phone in her room. I asked him "would you do me a favor and go to her room and call me from there?" He quizzically asked me "why?" I told him that I would like to speak with her. He reiterated that she was totally incoherent and could not communicate. I persisted and said "please Joe, indulge me and just try." I knew my request was weird but I uttered a quick prayer to the Lord. Joe reluctantly agreed. I thanked him and hung up the phone. As soon as I hung up, I made a mad dash to the men's room. After determining that the men's room was vacant, I went into a stall and prayed the most urgent prayer that I could. The fervency of that prayer practically rivaled the prayer Jesus prayed in Gethsemane minus the sweat and blood. I knew that the Holy Spirit was fueling the prayer. I said "Lord, this lady only has a short time to live and I don't think that she knows you. Please, Lord, touch her mind and give her awareness and let her be able to converse with me. I only need about ten minutes. I want to tell her about you. Give her back a lucid mind and a mind to believe in you and to give her heart to you. Father, she needs a miracle. Please, Lord, don't let her go to hell. In Jesus name I pray." Then I ran back to my work station. I literally felt like I was in a foot race against time, death and Satan. But I knew that the resources of heaven were with me.

As soon as I returned to my work station, my telephone was already ringing. It was Joe. Excitedly, Joe said "Mr. Watson, you won't believe this but she's awake and as aware as you and I. She's communicating normally!" I replied "I know. Quickly, put her on the telephone." From the reports I knew all about her life and medical condition and it was a tragic profile. She was a drug addict and prostitute. She abandoned her children and was completely alone. She stole whatever she could from whomever she could. And the poor thing was nothing but skin and bones; completely emaciated. She got on the phone.

When I heard that woman's voice my heart leaped into my throat. On the other end of the line, the voice I heard was angelic. It sounded so innocent and kind giving no hint to the hardness of her life. In fact, she sounded like a teenager instead of someone thirty-one years old. I felt God's love and compassion flowing through me, into the phone and right into her heart. I introduced myself and told her that I approved her claim and that all of her medical bills would be paid. She said "oh thank you Mr. Watson, you are so kind." The lump in my throat thickened. Then I asked her if I could speak personally to her. "Our business is over but I would like to speak to you about a personal matter. May I?" She replied "of course Mr. Watson."

I said "Miss, are you aware of how serious your condition is? She softly and sadly replied "yes I am." Then I asked "do you believe in God?" She said "yes I do." I asked her if she believed in heaven and hell. She did. I asked "which one do you think you will go to?" She spoke the following heart breaking words: "Mr. Watson, I know I am going to hell." Her voice broke. I told her that "God deeply loves you and does not want you to go to that horrible place." She replied "Mr Watson, you don't know the life that I've lived. God could not want someone as bad as I." With a breaking heart I said "Oh no, God wants you more than you can know and He will accept you just the way you are." She replied "Mr. Watson, you don't know all the things that I have done. No way God would want someone like me." Struggling to hold back my own tears, I told her "I know all about the prostitution, the drugs, crime, abandoned children and everything. But we are all sinners. You are not much worse than I. God still loves you more than all of the love in the world combined. It is He who sends me to you now. He wants you and sent me to bring you to Him." Then she started crying and asked "do you really think so Mr. Watson?" I answered "No, I absolutely know so." Weeping but with a glimmer of hope she whispered the question "You mean I could go to heaven?" I emphatically answered "Yes!!"

I then asked her if she believed that Jesus is the son of God. Without hesitation she replied "oh yes I do." I asked her "do you believe that He died for our sins and rose from the dead three days later?" She answered "Yes, that's what I was taught as a child and I always believed it." I told her that "There's your proof that God wants you because you could not believe that unless He allowed you to believe it." Then I asked "Are you willing to give your heart to Him now?" She quickly and forcefully replied "Yes!!" I then quoted and explained a couple scriptures to her (Romans 10:9&10, John 3:16). Then I explained to her that "It's not what one does that gets one into heaven; it's what one believes. Salvation is not a reward for a life well-lived; it is a gift for anyone who believes that Jesus is the son of God, died for our sins and was resurrected. One needs only to give their heart to Jesus and receive Him as their Lord and Savior. Right now, over the phone, we can say a simple prayer and, if you really mean it, you will be saved before we hang up the phone. Are you willing to pray with me right now?" With a new and unbridled hope she practically shouted "Yes, I will!" Oh the glory of that moment.

Then I led her in a short but powerful prayer of faith to God. Confessing that she was a sinner, she acknowledged Jesus as Lord, gave her heart to Him and received the gift of eternal life. After we prayed, she melted into a sea of tears. The weight of years of sins and guilt drained out in her tears; it was a soul cleansing cry. Silently, I wept with her. After several moments passed by, I told her "you are now my sister in Christ and your name is written in God's Book of Life. If you or I died right now we would go straight to heaven." I told her that "God loves you and I love you;" words I'm sure she hadn't heard in years. She laughed, cried and laughed again. It was beyond beautiful. It was heavenly. I could almost hear the sounds of our angels rejoicing. I merged my joy and tears with hers'. Most beautiful of all was that the Trinity was weeping and laughing with us.

Then I asked her "Would you like for me to visit you this weekend at the hospital?" She asked "You would do that for me Mr. Watson?" I replied "Only if you call me Lance." She giggled and said she would love for me to visit her. I told her I would come Saturday. We said a few more words then I prayed for her children and we hung up.

As I was sitting at my desk, totally detached from my surroundings and basking in the joy of what just transpired, my phone rang. It was Joe from the hospital. He asked "Mr. Watson, may I ask you a personal question?" I said "Of course." He asked me if I were a Christian. I affirmed that I was. Then he said "I heard her answers to your questions and I heard her praying with you. There was such life and joy in her face." Then I asked Joe if he were a Christian. He said that he was. I asked him if he ever spoke to her about salvation. He answered "I wanted to but that is strictly forbidden and I could lose my job." Incredulous, anger instantly arose in me and I told him "I could lose my job as well. How could you be silent? Her soul was at stake and you know that she only has a short time to live. God will protect you as He does me, but even if He chooses not to, He will open another door for you. You cannot compare your job security to her lost eternity. Are you seriously willing to protect your job and let her go to hell?" Joe was silent and I mentally rebuked myself for speaking so harshly to him. Then in a more gentle tone, I told him "Look Joe, God knows that you wanted to speak to her. He understands your fear. He did use you by having you call me at just the right moment. He allowed you to witness the miracle of her restored mind; you were an eye witness to her salvation. Let this be a lesson to you and learn well from it, for surely God will give you another opportunity. Remember Joe, that the stakes are just too high. I would be willing to lose a thousand jobs to see just one soul come to Christ." After an awkward silence, Joe said "I'm so glad I witnessed this. You don't know how this has affected me. Thanks Mr. Watson." On that note we ended our conversation.

Now the story gets freaky. I began to write up the claim when I suddenly noticed in the left side of the file papers that I hadn't noticed until that moment. This amazed me because I always read every single report in the file before I began any work on the claim. But I had not noticed these papers before that moment. I began to read them and I was totally shocked. I discovered the old close out report and saw that my signature was on it! I had this claim before! But how could that be because the computer never assigned a case twice to the same adjudicator? This was the first time in my two year employment with the agency that this occurred. Now, writing this twenty plus years later and having retired, it was the only time that I was assigned the same case twice.

This was Helen's claim!!! I couldn't believe it. That woman who I could not find eight months earlier was the very same woman I just prayed with!!! God hid this from me until that very moment! Then I remembered my prayer eight months ago for Helen. I had asked God to send her someone that really knew and loved him to tell her about Jesus. Eight months later God answered my prayer by sending Helen's claim back to me!!! Yet, He hid this from me until just that moment. This revelation so completely blew me away. I was stunned; the surroundings became surreal. I could not contain myself. I had to go to the bathroom and just, well, just get alone with my Lord and quietly weep. All I could say to the Lord was "Thank you, Lord. *THANK YOU*!!!"

As promised, that Saturday I went to the hospital to visit Helen. I was so anxious to meet her. I wanted to behold the face of the person who was the focal point of such extraordinary and amazing heavenly ordained developments. I went to the front desk and ask the attendant what room Helen was in; I knew that she was in quarantine. The attendant asked me if I was a relative. Silently, I said "Forgive me Lord," then I lied and said that I was. She told me that Helen died last night.

My heart exploded. I stepped back from the counter stunned, even devastated. In a semi-comatose state of mind, I drifted back to my car and wept like a baby for someone I never knew. I wept for someone who died so all alone and hated by so many. I wept because the Creator of all things, the One at the very summit of the universal food chain, the One who speaks worlds into existence went after Helen as a love-struck man would do for his beloved betrothed. God went after her with such a fervency, even though Helen was someone man would consider a total loser; someone that I would have nothing to do with. Someone nobody wanted or cared about. What manner of love is this? God mobilized all the resources of heaven to pursue a woman that mankind would discard in a moment! The words "How great thou art" took on a whole new meaning for me. And He used me.

Serving God is such a thrilling and incredible adventure. We belong to a God who truly loves the unlovable. God taught Joe a lesson. But God also taught me a lesson. No matter the cost, no matter the dangers and no matter how wretched the soul, pursue that soul with the gospel.

Lance Watson

My friend, I hope you enjoyed this true story about Helen. I can't wait to meet her in Heaven. Please pray for Helen's children. I don't know their names but God does. Pray for the salvation of Helen's children. Twenty-five years later I still, every day, pray for her children. And I know that I will have the joy one day of witnessing Helen's reunification with her children in heaven. God speed that day.

I have been a Christian for over three decades. God has used me to lead about three-hundred souls to Christ, all one-on-one. The adventures I have been on with God are breath-taking, thrilling and so, so fulfilling. The adventure of Helen is but one of so many adventures. There is no greater joy than partnering with God as He fervently pursues a lost soul. What about you? Do you know this joy? Do you want to? The only requirement is that you be saved and have a willing heart. Just ask the Lord to give you the boldness and opportunity to join Him as He searches out that lost sheep. Just ask Jesus. He will do it. And when He does, hold on tight and brace yourself for an adventure that only God can orchestrate. He will leave you breathless.

Printed in the United States
By Bookmasters